MW01717308

Just The
facts101
Textbook Key Facts

Textbook Outlines, Highlights, and Practice Quizzes

Principles of Managerial Finance, Brief

by Lawrence J. Gitman, 7th Edition

All "Just the Facts101" Material Written or Prepared by Cram101 Textbook Reviews

---

Title Page

WHY STOP HERE... THERE'S MORE ONLINE

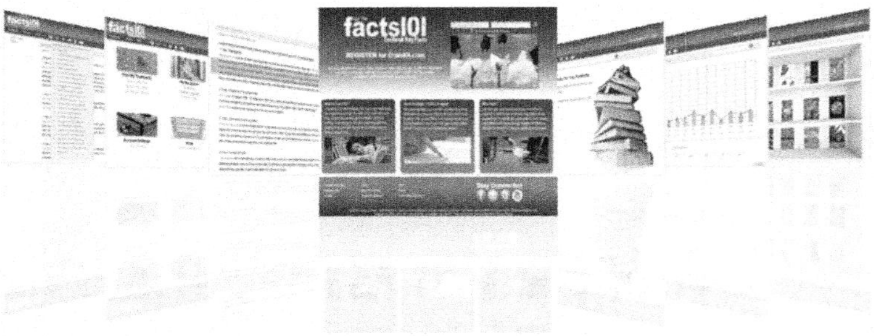

With technology and experience, we've developed tools that make studying easier and efficient. Like this Facts101 textbook notebook, **JustTheFactsl0l.com** offers you the highlights from every chapter of your actual textbook. However, unlike this notebook, **JustTheFactsl0l.com** gives you practice tests for each of the chapters. You also get access to in-depth reference material for writing essays and papers.

JustTheFactsl0l.COM FEATURES:

Outlines & Highlights
Just like the ones in this notebook, but with links to additional information.

Integrated Note Taking
Add your class notes to the Facts101 notes, print them and maximize your study time.

Problem Solving
Step-by-step walk throughs for math, stats and other disciplines.

Practice Exams
Five different test taking formats for every chapter.

Easy Access
Study any of your books, on any computer, anywhere.

Unlimited Textbooks
All the features above for virtually all your textbooks, just add them to your account at no additional cost.

Be sure to use the promo code above when registering on JustTheFactsl0l.com to get 50% off your membership fees.

STUDYING MADE EASY

This Factsl0l notebook is designed to make studying easier and increase your comprehension of the textbook material. Instead of starting with a blank notebook and trying to write down everything discussed in class lectures, you can use this Factsl0l textbook notebook and annotate your notes along with the lecture.

Our goal is to give you the best tools for success.

For a supreme understanding of the course, pair your notebook with our online tools. Should you decide you prefer jtfl0l.com as your study tool,

we'd like to offer you a trade...

Our Trade In program is a simple way for us to keep our promise and provide you the best studying tools, regardless of where you purchased your Factsl0l textbook notebook. As long as your notebook is in *Like New Condition**, you can send it back to us and we will immediately give you a JustTheFactsl0l.com account free for 120 days!

Let The **Trade In** *Begin!*

THREE SIMPLE STEPS TO TRADE:

1. Go to www.jtf101.com/tradein and fill out the packing slip information.
2. Submit and print the packing slip and mail it in with your Factsl0l textbook notebook.
3. Activate your account after you receive your email confirmation.

* Books must be returned in *Like New Condition*, meaning there is no damage to the book including, but not limited to; ripped or torn pages, markings or writing on pages, or folded / creased pages. Upon receiving the book, Factsl0l will inspect it and reserves the right to terminate your free Factsl0l.com account and return your textbook notebook at the owners expense.

facts101
LEARNING SYSTEM

"Just the Facts101" is a Content Technologies publication and tool designed to give you all the facts from your textbooks. Visit JustTheFacts101.com for the full practice test for each of your chapters for virtually any of your textbooks.

Facts101 has built custom study tools specific to your textbook. We provide all of the factual testable information and unlike traditional study guides, we will never send you back to your textbook for more information.

YOU WILL NEVER HAVE TO HIGHLIGHT A BOOK AGAIN!

Facts101 StudyGuides
All of the information in this StudyGuide is written specifically for your textbook. We include the key terms, places, people, and concepts... the information you can expect on your next exam!

Want to take a practice test?
Throughout each chapter of this StudyGuide you will find links to JustTheFacts101.com where you can select specific chapters to take a complete test on, or you can subscribe and get practice tests for up to 12 of your textbooks, along with other exclusive Jtf101.com tools like problem solving labs and reference libraries.

JustTheFacts101.com
Only Jtf101.com gives you the outlines, highlights, and PRACTICE TESTS specific to your textbook. JustTheFacts101.com is an online application where you'll discover study tools designed to make the most of your limited study time.

By purchasing this book, you get 50% off the normal monthly subscription fee!. Just enter the promotional code **'DK73DW24583'** on the Jtf101.com registration screen.

www.JustTheFacts101.com

Copyright © 2014 by Content Technologies, Inc. All rights reserved.
"Just the FACTS101"®, "Cram101"® and "Never Highlight a Book Again!"® are registered trademarks of Content Technologies, Inc.
ISBN(s): 9781490299655. PUBE-1.201469

facts101

Principles of Managerial Finance, Brief
Lawrence J. Gitman, 7th

CONTENTS

1. The Role of Managerial Finance

CHAPTER OUTLINE: KEY TERMS, PEOPLE, PLACES, CONCEPTS

- Managerial finance
- Financial services
- Articles of partnership
- General partnership
- Board of directors
- Common stock
- Dividend
- Limited liability
- Limited liability company
- Limited liability partnership
- Limited partnership
- Earnings per share
- Shadow banking
- Cash flow
- Business ethics
- Stakeholder
- Tax cut
- Sarbanes-Oxley Act
- Debt-to-equity ratio
- Corporate governance
- Institutional investor

1. The Role of Managerial Finance

CHAPTER HIGHLIGHTS & NOTES: KEY TERMS, PEOPLE, PLACES, CONCEPTS

Managerial finance	Managerial finance is the branch of finance that concerns itself with the managerial significance of finance techniques. It is focused on assessment rather than technique. The difference between a managerial and a technical approach can be seen in the questions one might ask of annual reports.
Financial services	Financial services are the economic services provided by the finance industry, which encompasses a broad range of organizations that manage money, including credit unions, banks, credit card companies, insurance companies, accountancy companies, consumer finance companies, stock brokerages, investment funds and some government sponsored enterprises. As of 2004, the financial services industry represented 20% of the market capitalization of the S&P 500 in the United States. The U.S. finance industry comprised only 10% of total non-farm business profits in 1947, but it grew to 50% by 2010. Over the same period, finance industry income as a proportion of GDP rose from 2.5% to 7.5%, and the finance industry's proportion of all corporate income rose from 10% to 20%.
Articles of partnership	Articles of partnership is a voluntary contract between two or among more than two persons to place their capital, labor, and skills, and corporation in business with the understanding that there will be a sharing of the profits and losses between/among partners. Outside of North America, it is normally referred to simply as a partnership agreement.
General partnership	In the commercial and legal parlance of most countries, a general partnership, refers to an association of persons or an unincorporated company with the following major features: It is a partnership in which partners share equally in both responsibility and liability.
Board of directors	A board of directors is a body of elected or appointed members who jointly oversee the activities of a company or organization. Other names include board of governors, board of managers, board of regents, board of trustees, and board of visitors. It is often simply referred to as 'the board'.
Common stock	Common stock is a form of corporate equity ownership, a type of security. The terms 'voting share' or 'ordinary share' are also used in other parts of the world; common stock being primarily used in the United States. It is called 'common' to distinguish it from preferred stock.
Dividend	A dividend is a payment made by a corporation to its shareholders, usually as a distribution of profits. When a corporation earns a profit or surplus, it can either re-invest it in the business (called retained earnings), or it can distribute it to shareholders. A corporation may retain a portion of its earnings and pay the remainder as a dividend.

Limited liability	Limited liability is a concept whereby a person's financial liability is limited to a fixed sum, most commonly the value of a person's investment in a company or partnership with limited liability. If a company with limited liability is sued, then the plaintiffs are suing the company, not its owners or investors. A shareholder in a limited company is not personally liable for any of the debts of the company, other than for the value of their investment in that company.
Limited liability company	A limited liability company is a flexible form of enterprise that blends elements of partnership and corporate structures. An Limited liability company is not a corporation; it is a legal form of company that provides limited liability to its owners in the vast majority of United States jurisdictions. Limited liability companys do not need to be organized for profit.
Limited liability partnership	A limited liability partnership is a partnership in which some or all partners (depending on the jurisdiction) have limited liability. It therefore exhibits elements of partnerships and corporations. In an Limited liability partnership, one partner is not responsible or liable for another partner's misconduct or negligence.
Limited partnership	A limited partnership is a form of partnership similar to a general partnership, except that in addition to one or more general partners, there are one or more limited partners (LPs). It is a partnership in which only one partner is required to be a general partner. The GPs are, in all major respects, in the same legal position as partners in a conventional firm, i.e. they have management control, share the right to use partnership property, share the profits of the firm in predefined proportions, and have joint and several liability for the debts of the partnership.
Earnings per share	Earnings per share are the amount of earnings of each outstanding share of a company's stock. The Financial Accounting Standards Board (FASB) requires companies' income statements to report Earnings per share for each major category of the income statement: continuing operations, discontinued operations, extraordinary items and net income.
Shadow banking	The shadow banking system is the collection of non-bank financial intermediaries that provide services similar to traditional commercial banks. It is sometimes said to include entities such as hedge funds, money market funds and structured investment vehicles (SIV), but the meaning and scope of shadow banking is disputed in the academic literature. Investment banks as well as commercial banks may conduct much of their business in the shadow banking system (SBS), but most are not generally classed as SBS institutions themselves.
Cash flow	Cash flow is the movement of money into or out of a business, project, or financial product. It is usually measured during a specified, limited period of time. Measurement of cash flow can be used for calculating other parameters that give information on a company's value and situation.

1. The Role of Managerial Finance

CHAPTER HIGHLIGHTS & NOTES: KEY TERMS, PEOPLE, PLACES, CONCEPTS

Business ethics	Business ethics is a form of applied ethics or professional ethics that examines ethical principles and moral or ethical problems that arise in a business environment. It applies to all aspects of business conduct and is relevant to the conduct of individuals and entire organizations. Business ethics has both normative and descriptive dimensions.
Stakeholder	A corporate stakeholder is a party that can affect or be affected by the actions of the business as a whole. The stakeholder concept was first used in a 1963 internal memorandum at the Stanford Research Institute. It defined stakeholders as 'those groups without whose support the organization would cease to exist.' The theory was later developed and championed by R. Edward Freeman in the 1980s.
Tax cut	A tax cut is a reduction in taxes. The immediate effects of a tax cut are a decrease in the real income of the government and an increase in the real income of those whose tax rate has been lowered. Due to the perceived benefit in growing real incomes among tax payers politicians have sought to claim their proposed tax credits as tax cuts.
Sarbanes-Oxley Act	The Sarbanes-Oxley Act of 2002 (Pub.L. 107-204, 116 Stat. 745, enacted July 29, 2002), also known as the 'Public Company Accounting Reform and Investor Protection Act' (in the Senate) and 'Corporate and Auditing Accountability and Responsibility Act' (in the House) and more commonly called Sarbanes-Oxley, Sarbox or SOX, is a United States federal law that set new or enhanced standards for all U.S. public company boards, management and public accounting firms. ponsors U.S. Senator Paul Sarbanes (D-MD) and U.S. Representative Michael G. Oxley (R-OH). As a result of SOX, top management must now individually certify the accuracy of financial information.
Debt-to-equity ratio	The debt-to-equity ratio is a financial ratio indicating the relative proportion of shareholders' equity and debt used to finance a company's assets. Closely related to leveraging, the ratio is also known as Risk, Gearing or Leverage. The two components are often taken from the firm's balance sheet or statement of financial position (so-called book value), but the ratio may also be calculated using market values for both, if the company's debt and equity are publicly traded, or using a combination of book value for debt and market value for equity financially.
Corporate governance	Corporate governance refers to the system by which corporations are directed and controlled. The governance structure specifies the distribution of rights and responsibilities among different participants in the corporation (such as the board of directors, managers, shareholders, creditors, auditors, regulators, and other stakeholders) and specifies the rules and procedures for making decisions in corporate affairs. Governance provides the structure through which corporations set and pursue their objectives, while reflecting the context of the social, regulatory and market environment.
Institutional investor	Institutional investors are organizations which pool large sums of money and invest those sums in securities, real property and other investment assets.

CHAPTER HIGHLIGHTS & NOTES: KEY TERMS, PEOPLE, PLACES, CONCEPTS

They can also include operating companies which decide to invest their profits to some degree in these types of assets.

Typical investors include banks, insurance companies, retirement or pension funds, hedge funds, investment advisors and mutual funds.

CHAPTER QUIZ: KEY TERMS, PEOPLE, PLACES, CONCEPTS

1. A _________ is a reduction in taxes. The immediate effects of a _________ are a decrease in the real income of the government and an increase in the real income of those whose tax rate has been lowered. Due to the perceived benefit in growing real incomes among tax payers politicians have sought to claim their proposed tax credits as _________s.

   a. Tax cut
   b. Tax deferral
   c. Tax expense
   d. Tax exporting

2. In the commercial and legal parlance of most countries, a C_________, refers to an association of persons or an unincorporated company with the following major features:

   It is a partnership in which partners share equally in both responsibility and liability.

   a. Limited liability partnership
   b. limited partner
   c. General partnership
   d. granularity

3. The _________ is a financial ratio indicating the relative proportion of shareholders' equity and debt used to finance a company's assets. Closely related to leveraging, the ratio is also known as Risk, Gearing or Leverage. The two components are often taken from the firm's balance sheet or statement of financial position (so-called book value), but the ratio may also be calculated using market values for both, if the company's debt and equity are publicly traded, or using a combination of book value for debt and market value for equity financially.

   a. Debt-to-GDP ratio
   b. Debt-to-equity ratio
   c. Debtor collection period
   d. Diluted earnings per share

4. A __a__ is a form of partnership similar to a general partnership, except that in addition to one or more general partners, there are one or more limited partners (LPs). It is a partnership in which only one partner is required to be a general partner.

   The GPs are, in all major respects, in the same legal position as partners in a conventional firm, i.e. they have management control, share the right to use partnership property, share the profits of the firm in predefined proportions, and have joint and several liability for the debts of the partnership.

   a. Limited partnership
   b. Negative option billing
   c. Novated lease
   d. Novation

5. __C__ are the economic services provided by the finance industry, which encompasses a broad range of organizations that manage money, including credit unions, banks, credit card companies, insurance companies, accountancy companies, consumer finance companies, stock brokerages, investment funds and some government sponsored enterprises.

   As of 2004, the __c__ industry represented 20% of the market capitalization of the S&P 500 in the United States. The U.S. finance industry comprised only 10% of total non-farm business profits in 1947, but it grew to 50% by 2010. Over the same period, finance industry income as a proportion of GDP rose from 2.5% to 7.5%, and the finance industry's proportion of all corporate income rose from 10% to 20%.

   a. Fundamentally based indexes
   b. Fundo de Investimento em Direitos Creditrios
   c. Financial services
   d. Big boy letter

ANSWER KEY
1. The Role of Managerial Finance

1. a
2. c
3. b
4. a
5. c

You can take the complete Chapter Practice Test

for 1. The Role of Managerial Finance
on all key terms, persons, places, and concepts.

Online 99 Cents

http://www.JustTheFacts101.com

Use www.JustTheFacts101.com for all your study needs

including Facts101's online interactive problem solving labs in

chemistry, statistics, mathematics, and more.

2. The Financial Market Environment

CHAPTER OUTLINE: KEY TERMS, PEOPLE, PLACES, CONCEPTS

- Financial institution
- Commercial bank
- Glass-Steagall Act
- Investment bank
- Shadow banking
- Shadow banking system
- Financial market
- Primary market
- Private placement
- Public offering
- Secondary market
- Flow of Funds
- Capital market
- Money market
- Common stock
- Market maker
- Preferred stock
- Ask price
- Bid price
- International Capital Markets
- Behavioral Finance

2. The Financial Market Environment

CHAPTER OUTLINE: KEY TERMS, PEOPLE, PLACES, CONCEPTS

- ______ Mortgage-backed security
- ______ Securitization
- ______ Great Recession
- ______ Consumer protection
- ______ Gramm-Leach-Bliley Act
- ______ Dividend policy
- ______ Average tax rate
- ______ Ordinary income
- ______ Deductible expense
- ______ Dividend
- ______ Capital gain

CHAPTER HIGHLIGHTS & NOTES: KEY TERMS, PEOPLE, PLACES, CONCEPTS

Financial institution

In financial economics, a financial institution is an institution that provides financial services for its clients or members. Probably the most important financial service provided by financial institutions is acting as financial intermediaries. Most financial institutions are regulated by the government.

Commercial bank

A commercial bank is a type of financial institution and intermediary. It is a bank that provides transactional, savings, and money market accounts and that accepts time deposits.

After the implementation of the Glass-Steagall Act, the U.S. Congress required that banks engage only in banking activities, whereas investment banks were limited to capital market activities.

Glass-Steagall Act

The Glass-Steagall Act is a term often applied to the entire Banking Act of 1933, after its Congressional sponsors, Senator Carter Glass (D) of Virginia, and Representative Henry B.

Investment bank	An investment bank is a financial institution that assists individuals, corporations and governments in raising capital by underwriting and/or acting as the client's agent in the issuance of securities. An investment bank may also assist companies involved in mergers and acquisitions, and provide ancillary services such as market making, trading of derivatives, fixed income instruments, foreign exchange, commodities, and equity securities. Unlike commercial banks and retail banks, investment banks do not take deposits.
Shadow banking	The shadow banking system is the collection of non-bank financial intermediaries that provide services similar to traditional commercial banks. It is sometimes said to include entities such as hedge funds, money market funds and structured investment vehicles (SIV), but the meaning and scope of shadow banking is disputed in the academic literature. Investment banks as well as commercial banks may conduct much of their business in the shadow banking system (SBS), but most are not generally classed as SBS institutions themselves.
Shadow banking system	The shadow banking system is the collection of non-bank financial intermediaries that provide services similar to traditional commercial banks. It is sometimes said to include entities such as hedge funds, money market funds, structured investment vehicles (SIV), 'credit investment funds, exchange-traded funds, credit hedge funds, private equity funds, securities broker dealers, credit insurance providers, securitization and finance companies.'(Jones 2013) but the meaning and scope of shadow banking is disputed in academic literature. According to Hervé Hannoun, Deputy General Manager of the Bank for International Settlements(BIS), investment banks as well as commercial banks may conduct much of their business in the shadow banking system but most are not generally classed as Shadow banking system institutions themselves.(Hannoun 2008) At least one financial regulatory expert has said that regulated banking organizations are the largest shadow banks.
Financial market	A financial market is a market in which people and entities can trade financial securities, commodities, and other fungible items of value at low transaction costs and at prices that reflect supply and demand. Securities include stocks and bonds, and commodities include precious metals or agricultural goods. There are both general markets (where many commodities are traded) and specialized markets (where only one commodity is traded).
Primary market	The primary market is that part of the capital markets that deals with the issuance of new securities. Companies, governments or public sector institutions can obtain bonds through the sale of a new stock or bond issue. This is typically done through a syndicate of securities dealers.
Private placement	Private placement is a funding round of securities which are sold not through a public offering, but rather through a private offering, mostly to a small number of chosen investors.

'Private placement' usually refers to non-public offering of shares in a public company (since, of course, any offering of shares in a private company is and can only be a private offering).

PIPE (private investment in public equity) deals are one type of private placement.

Public offering	A public offering is the offering of securities of a company or a similar corporation to the public. Generally, the securities are to be listed on a stock exchange. In most jurisdictions, a public offering requires the issuing company to publish a prospectus detailing the terms and rights attached to the offered security, as well as information on the company itself and its finances.
Secondary market	The secondary market, also called aftermarket, is the financial market in which previously issued financial instruments such as stock, bonds, options, and futures are bought and sold. Another frequent usage of 'secondary market' is to refer to loans which are sold by a mortgage bank to investors such as Fannie Mae and Freddie Mac. The term 'secondary market' is also used to refer to the market for any used goods or assets, or an alternative use for an existing product or asset where the customer base is the second market (for example, corn has been traditionally used primarily for food production and feedstock, but a 'second' or 'third' market has developed for use in ethanol production).
Flow of Funds	The Flow of Funds, is an examination of a country's financial flows, usually conducted by the country's monetary authority or central bank. In the United States, the Flow of Funds section of the Federal Reserve is responsible for tracking these financial flows. The Federal Reserve publishes the results as a Federal Reserve Statistical Release called the U.S. Flow of Funds Accounts every quarter.
Capital market	Capital markets are financial markets for the buying and selling of long-term debt- or equity-backed securities. These markets channel the wealth of savers to those who can put it to long-term productive use, such as companies or governments making long-term investments. Financial regulators, such as the UK's Bank of England (BoE) or the U.S. Securities and Exchange Commission (SEC), oversee the capital markets in their jurisdictions to protect investors against fraud, among other duties.
Money market	As money became a commodity, the money market became a component of the financial markets for assets involved in short-term borrowing, lending, buying and selling with original maturities of one year or less. Trading in the money markets is done over the counter and is wholesale. Various instruments exist, such as Treasury bills, commercial paper, bankers' acceptances, deposits, certificates of deposit, bills of exchange, repurchase agreements, federal funds, and short-lived mortgage-, and asset-backed securities.
Common stock	Common stock is a form of corporate equity ownership, a type of security.

The terms 'voting share' or 'ordinary share' are also used in other parts of the world; common stock being primarily used in the United States.

It is called 'common' to distinguish it from preferred stock.

Market maker

A market maker is a company, or an individual, that quotes both a buy and a sell price in a financial instrument or commodity held in inventory, hoping to make a profit on the bid-offer spread, or turn.

Preferred stock

Preferred stock is an equity security which may have any combination of features not possessed by common stock including properties of both an equity and a debt instruments, and is generally considered a hybrid instrument. Preferreds are senior (i.e. higher ranking) to common stock, but subordinate to bonds in terms of claim .

Preferred stock usually carries no voting rights, but may carry a dividend and may have priority over common stock in the payment of dividends and upon liquidation.

Ask price

Ask price, also called offer price, offer, asking price, or simply ask, is the price a seller states she or he will accept for a good.

The seller may qualify the stated asking price as firm or negotiable. Firm means the seller is saying he or she won't change the price.

Bid price

A bid price is the highest price that a buyer is willing to pay for a good. It is usually referred to simply as the 'bid.'

In bid and ask, the bid price stands in contrast to the ask price or 'offer', and the difference between the two is called the bid/ask spread.

An unsolicited bid or purchase offer is when a person or company receives a bid even though they are not looking to sell.

International Capital Markets

International Capital Markets, commonly known as 'International Capital Markets' or 'IC Markets' is an Australian based investment company offering over-the-counter (OTC) and exchange traded derivative products including direct market access (DMA) Contracts-For-Difference (CFDs), foreign exchange (Forex) and global futures contracts to its retail and professional client base. International Capital Markets is one of Australia's largest CFD and Forex providers.

Clients

The Group's client base is dominated by retail clients, particularly in its CFD and Forex business.

2. The Financial Market Environment

CHAPTER HIGHLIGHTS & NOTES: KEY TERMS, PEOPLE, PLACES, CONCEPTS

Behavioral Finance	Behavioral economics and the related field, behavioral finance, study the effects of social, cognitive, and emotional factors on the economic decisions of individuals and institutions and the consequences for market prices, returns, and the resource allocation. The fields are primarily concerned with the bounds of rationality of economic agents. Behavioral models typically integrate insights from psychology with neo-classical economic theory.
Mortgage-backed security	A mortgage-backed security is a type of asset-backed security that is secured by a mortgage, or more commonly a collection ('pool') of sometimes hundreds of mortgages. The mortgages are sold to a financial institution (a government agency or investment bank) that 'securitizes', or packages, the loans together into a security that can be sold to investors. The mortgages of a Mortgage backed security may be residential or commercial; in the United States they may issued by structures set up by government-sponsored enterprises like Fannie Mae or Freddie Mac, or they can be 'private-label', issued by structures set up by investment banks.
Securitization	Securitization is the financial practice of pooling various types of contractual debt, such as residential mortgages, commercial mortgages, auto loans, or credit card debt obligations, and selling said consolidated debt as pass-through securities, or collateralized mortgage obligation to various investors. The cash collected from the financial instruments underlying the security is paid to the various investors who had advance money for that right. Securities backed by residential mortgage receivables are called residential-mortgage-backed securities (RMBS), while those backed by other types of receivables are asset-backed securities (ABS).
Great Recession	The Great Recession is a marked global economic decline that began in December 2007 and took a particularly sharp downward turn in September 2008. The initial phase of the ongoing crisis, which manifested as a liquidity crisis, can be dated from August 7, 2007, when BNP Paribas, citing a 'complete evaporation of liquidity,' terminated withdrawals from three hedge funds. The bursting of the U.S. housing bubble, which peaked in 2006, caused the values of securities tied to U.S. real estate pricing to plummet, damaging financial institutions globally. The global recession has affected the entire world economy, with greater detriment to some countries than others.
Consumer protection	Consumer protection is a group of laws and organizations designed to ensure the rights of consumers as well as fair trade competition and the free flow of truthful information in the marketplace. The laws are designed to prevent businesses that engage in fraud or specified unfair practices from gaining an advantage over competitors; they may also provide additional protection for the weak and those unable to take care of themselves. Consumer protection laws are a form of government regulation, which aim to protect the rights of consumers.
Gramm-Leach-Bliley Act	The Gramm-Leach-Bliley Act also known as the Financial Services Modernization Act of 1999, (Pub.L. 106-102, 113 Stat. 1338, enacted November 12, 1999) is an act of the 106th United States Congress (1999-2001).

It repealed part of the Glass-Steagall Act of 1933, removing barriers in the market among banking companies, securities companies and insurance companies that prohibited any one institution from acting as any combination of an investment bank, a commercial bank, and an insurance company. With the passage of the Gramm-Leach-Bliley Act, commercial banks, investment banks, securities firms, and insurance companies were allowed to consolidate.

Dividend policy

Dividend policy is concerned with financial policies regarding paying cash dividend in the present or paying an increased dividend at a later stage. Whether to issue dividends, and what amount, is determined mainly on the basis of the company's unappropriated profit (excess cash) and influenced by the company's long-term earning power. When cash surplus exists and is not needed by the firm, then management is expected to pay out some or all of those surplus earnings in the form of cash dividends or to repurchase the company's stock through a share buyback program.

Average tax rate

Average tax rate is the average percent you pay in taxes out of your taxable income, based upon the tax brackets you fall into. For example: John Doe files taxes as a single man, with a total of $65,000 in taxable income. The first $7,550 he made would be taxed at 10%, then income between $7,550 and $30,650 would be taxed at 15%, with the remainder taxed at 25%.

Ordinary income

Under the United States Internal Revenue Code, the type of income is defined by its character. Ordinary income is usually characterized as income other than capital gain. Ordinary income can consist of income from wages, salaries, tips, commissions, bonuses, and other types of compensation from employment, interest, dividends, or net income from a sole proprietorship, partnership or LLC. Rents and royalties, after certain deductions, depreciation or depletion allowances, and gambling winnings are also treated as ordinary income.

Deductible expense

A tax deduction or a tax-Deductible expense affects a taxpayer's income tax. A tax deduction represents an expense incurred by a taxpayer. They are variable amounts that you can subtract, or deduct, from your gross income.It is subtracted from gross income when the taxpayer computes his or her income taxes.

Dividend

A dividend is a payment made by a corporation to its shareholders, usually as a distribution of profits. When a corporation earns a profit or surplus, it can either re-invest it in the business (called retained earnings), or it can distribute it to shareholders. A corporation may retain a portion of its earnings and pay the remainder as a dividend.

Capital gain

A capital gain is a profit that results from a disposition of a capital asset, such as stock, bond or real estate, where the amount realized on the disposition exceeds the purchase price. The gain is the difference between a higher selling price and a lower purchase price. Conversely, a capital loss arises if the proceeds from the sale of a capital asset are less than the purchase price.

2. The Financial Market Environment

CHAPTER QUIZ: KEY TERMS, PEOPLE, PLACES, CONCEPTS

1. A _________ is a payment made by a corporation to its shareholders, usually as a distribution of profits. When a corporation earns a profit or surplus, it can either re-invest it in the business (called retained earnings), or it can distribute it to shareholders. A corporation may retain a portion of its earnings and pay the remainder as a _________.

   a. Bonus share
   b. Common stock dividend
   c. Dividend
   d. Dividend cover

2. A tax deduction or a tax-_________ affects a taxpayer's income tax. A tax deduction represents an expense incurred by a taxpayer. They are variable amounts that you can subtract, or deduct, from your gross income.It is subtracted from gross income when the taxpayer computes his or her income taxes.

   a. Recourse debt
   b. Ecotax
   c. Effective marginal tax rate
   d. Deductible expense

3. _________ is a form of corporate equity ownership, a type of security. The terms 'voting share' or 'ordinary share' are also used in other parts of the world; _________ being primarily used in the United States.

   It is called 'common' to distinguish it from preferred stock.

   a. Common stock
   b. Control premium
   c. Corporate synergy
   d. Critical accounting policy

4. Behavioral economics and the related field, _________, study the effects of social, cognitive, and emotional factors on the economic decisions of individuals and institutions and the consequences for market prices, returns, and the resource allocation. The fields are primarily concerned with the bounds of rationality of economic agents. Behavioral models typically integrate insights from psychology with neo-classical economic theory.

   a. Behavioral Finance
   b. Self-fulfilling prophecy
   c. granularity
   d. Collateral

5. . Under the United States Internal Revenue Code, the type of income is defined by its character. _________ is usually characterized as income other than capital gain. _________ can consist of income from wages, salaries, tips, commissions, bonuses, and other types of compensation from employment, interest, dividends, or net income from a sole proprietorship, partnership or LLC. Rents and royalties, after certain deductions, depreciation or depletion allowances, and gambling winnings are also treated as _________.

a. Efficiency Based Absorption Costing
b. Ecotax
c. Ordinary income
d. Effective rate of protection

ANSWER KEY
2. The Financial Market Environment

---

1. c
2. d
3. a
4. a
5. c

You can take the complete Chapter Practice Test

for 2. The Financial Market Environment
on all key terms, persons, places, and concepts.

Online 99 Cents

http://www.JustTheFacts101.com

Use www.JustTheFacts101.com for all your study needs

including Facts101's online interactive problem solving labs in

chemistry, statistics, mathematics, and more.

3. Financial Statements and Ratio Analysis

CHAPTER OUTLINE: KEY TERMS, PEOPLE, PLACES, CONCEPTS

______ Financial Accounting Standards Board

______ Public company

______ Earnings per share

______ Asset

______ Face value

______ Ask price

______ Paid-in Capital

______ Retained earnings

______ Capital

______ Statement of retained earnings

______ Cash flow statement

______ Financial services

______ Notes to financial statements

______ Consolidation

______ Financial statement

______ Benchmarking

______ Cross-sectional studies

______ Ratio

______ Financial ratio

______ Current ratio

______ Quick ratio

3. Financial Statements and Ratio Analysis

CHAPTER OUTLINE: KEY TERMS, PEOPLE, PLACES, CONCEPTS

________	Inventory turnover
________	Stock market
________	Debt ratio
________	Debt-to-equity ratio
________	Gross profit
________	Accounting profit
________	Operating margin
________	Net profit
________	Net profit margin
________	Return on equity

CHAPTER HIGHLIGHTS & NOTES: KEY TERMS, PEOPLE, PLACES, CONCEPTS

Financial Accounting Standards Board

The Financial Accounting Standards Board is a private, not-for-profit organization whose primary purpose is to develop generally accepted accounting principles (GAAP) within the United States in the public's interest. The Securities and Exchange Commission (SEC) designated the Financial Accounting Standards Board as the organization responsible for setting accounting standards for public companies in the U.S. It was created in 1973, replacing the Committee on Accounting Procedure (CAP) and the Accounting Principles Board (APB) of the American Institute of Certified Public Accountants (AICPA).

Public company

This is not the same as a publicly owned enterprise or a government-owned corporation.

A public company, publicly traded company, publicly held company, or public limited company is a limited liability company that offers its securities (stock/shares, bonds/loans, etc). for sale to the general public, typically through a stock exchange, or through market makers operating in over the counter markets.

Earnings per share	Earnings per share are the amount of earnings of each outstanding share of a company's stock. The Financial Accounting Standards Board (FASB) requires companies' income statements to report Earnings per share for each major category of the income statement: continuing operations, discontinued operations, extraordinary items and net income.
Asset	In financial accounting, assets are economic resources. Anything tangible or intangible that is capable of being owned or controlled to produce value and that is held to have positive economic value is considered an asset. Simply stated, assets represent value of ownership that can be converted into cash (although cash itself is also considered an asset).
Face value	The face value is the value of a coin, stamp or paper money, as printed on the coin, stamp or bill itself by the minting authority. While the face value usually refers to the true value of the coin, stamp or bill in question (as with circulation coins) it can sometimes be largely symbolic, as is often the case with bullion coins. For example, a one troy ounce (31 g) American Gold Eagle bullion coin was worth and sold for about $1,200 USD during 2009 market prices (as of November 14, 2009) and yet has a face value of only $50 USD.
Ask price	Ask price, also called offer price, offer, asking price, or simply ask, is the price a seller states she or he will accept for a good. The seller may qualify the stated asking price as firm or negotiable. Firm means the seller is saying he or she won't change the price.
Paid-in Capital	(Paid-in capital or Contributed capital) refers to capital contributed to a corporation by investors through purchase of stock from the corporation (not through purchase of stock in the open market from other stockholders (secondary market)). It includes share capital (i.e. capital stock) as well as additional paid-in capital. The paid-in capital account does not reflect the amount of capital contributed by any specific investor.
Retained earnings	In accounting, retained earnings refers to the portion of net income of a corporation that is retained by the corporation rather than distributed to shareholders as dividends, or as the amount available to the corporation for distribution to shareholders. Similarly, if the corporation incurs a loss, then that loss reduces the corporation's retained earnings balance. If the balance of the retained earnings account is negative it may be called retained losses, accumulated losses or accumulated deficit, or similar terminology.
Capital	In economics, capital, capital goods, or real capital are those already-produced durable goods that are used in production of goods or services. The capital goods are not significantly consumed, though they may depreciate in the production process.

3. Financial Statements and Ratio Analysis

CHAPTER HIGHLIGHTS & NOTES: KEY TERMS, PEOPLE, PLACES, CONCEPTS

Statement of retained earnings	A statement of retained earnings is a basic financial statement. The statement explains the changes in a company's retained earnings over the reporting period. They break down changes in the owners' interest in the organization, and in the application of retained profit or surplus from one accounting period to the next.
Cash flow statement	In financial accounting, a cash flow statement, also known as statement of cash flows, is a financial statement that shows how changes in balance sheet accounts and income affect cash and cash equivalents, and breaks the analysis down to operating, investing, and financing activities. Essentially, the cash flow statement is concerned with the flow of cash in and out of the business. The statement captures both the current operating results and the accompanying changes in the balance sheet.
Financial services	Financial services are the economic services provided by the finance industry, which encompasses a broad range of organizations that manage money, including credit unions, banks, credit card companies, insurance companies, accountancy companies, consumer finance companies, stock brokerages, investment funds and some government sponsored enterprises. As of 2004, the financial services industry represented 20% of the market capitalization of the S&P 500 in the United States. The U.S. finance industry comprised only 10% of total non-farm business profits in 1947, but it grew to 50% by 2010. Over the same period, finance industry income as a proportion of GDP rose from 2.5% to 7.5%, and the finance industry's proportion of all corporate income rose from 10% to 20%.
Notes to financial statements	Notes to financial statements are additional information added to the end of financial statements. Notes to financial statements help explain specific items in the financial statements as well as provide a more comprehensive assessment of a company's financial condition. Notes to financial statements can include information on debt, going concern criteria, accounts, contingent liabilities or contextual information explaining the financial numbers (e.g. to indicate a lawsuit).
Consolidation	Consolidation or amalgamation is the act of merging many things into one. In business, it often refers to the mergers and acquisitions of many smaller companies into much larger ones. In the context of financial accounting, consolidation refers to the aggregation of financial statements of a group company as consolidated financial statements.
Financial statement	A financial statement is a formal record of the financial activities of a business, person, or other entity. Relevant financial information is presented in a structured manner and in a form easy to understand.

Benchmarking

Benchmarking is the process of comparing one's business processes and performance metrics to industry bests or best practices from other industries. Dimensions typically measured are quality, time and cost. In the process of best practice benchmarking, management identifies the best firms in their industry, or in another industry where similar processes exist, and compares the results and processes of those studied (the 'targets') to one's own results and processes.

Cross-sectional studies

Cross-sectional studies form a class of research methods that involve observation of all of a population, or a representative subset, at one specific point in time. They differ from case-control studies in that they aim to provide data on the entire population under study, whereas case-control studies typically include only individuals with a specific characteristic, with a sample, often a tiny minority, of the rest of the population. Cross-sectional studies are descriptive studies (neither longitudinal nor experimental).

Ratio

In mathematics, a ratio is a relationship between two numbers of the same kind (e.g., objects, persons, students, spoonfuls, units of whatever identical dimension), usually expressed as 'a to b' or a:b, sometimes expressed arithmetically as a dimensionless quotient of the two that explicitly indicates how many times the first number contains the second (not necessarily an integer).

In layman's terms a ratio represents, simply, for every amount of one thing, how much there is of another thing. For example, supposing one has 8 oranges and 6 lemons in a bowl of fruit, the ratio of oranges to lemons would be 4:3 (which is equivalent to 8:6) and the ratio of lemons to oranges would be would be 3:4. Additionally, the ratio of oranges to the total amount of fruit is 4:7 (equivalent to 8:14).

Financial ratio

A financial ratio is a relative magnitude of two selected numerical values taken from an enterprise's financial statements. Often used in accounting, there are many standard ratios used to try to evaluate the overall financial condition of a corporation or other organization. Financial ratios may be used by managers within a firm, by current and potential shareholders (owners) of a firm, and by a firm's creditors.

Current ratio

The current ratio is a financial ratio that measures whether or not a firm has enough resources to pay its debts over the next 12 months. It compares a firm's current assets to its current liabilities. It is expressed as follows:

$$\text{Current ratio} = \frac{\text{Current Assets}}{\text{Current Liabilities}}$$

The current ratio is an indication of a firm's market liquidity and ability to meet creditor's demands.

Quick ratio

In finance, the Acid-test or quick ratio or liquid ratio measures the ability of a company to use its near cash or quick assets to extinguish or retire its current liabilities immediately.

Quick assets include those current assets that presumably can be quickly converted to cash at close to their book values. A company with a Quick Ratio of less than 1 cannot currently pay back its current liabilities.

Inventory turnover

In accounting, the Inventory turnover is a measure of the number of times inventory is sold or used in a time period such as a year. The equation for inventory turnover equals the cost of goods sold divided by the average inventory. Inventory turnover is also known as inventory turns, stockturn, stock turns, turns, and stock turnover.

Stock market

A stock market or equity market is a public entity for the trading of company stock (shares) and derivatives at an agreed price; these are securities listed on a stock exchange as well as those only traded privately.

The size of the world stock market was estimated at about $36.6 trillion at the beginning of October 2008. The total world derivatives market has been estimated at about $791 trillion face or nominal value, 11 times the size of the entire world economy. The value of the derivatives market, because it is stated in terms of notional values, cannot be directly compared to a stock or a fixed income security, which traditionally refers to an actual value.

Debt ratio

Debt Ratio is a financial ratio that indicates the percentage of a company's assets that are provided via debt. It is the ratio of total debt (the sum of current liabilities and long-term liabilities) and total assets (the sum of current assets, fixed assets, and other assets such as 'goodwill').

$$\text{Debt ratio} = \frac{\text{Total Debt}}{\text{Total Assets}}$$

or alternatively:

$$\text{Debt ratio} = \frac{\text{Total Liability}}{\text{Total Assets}}$$

For example, a company with $2 million in total assets and $500,000 in total liabilities would have a debt ratio of 25%.

Debt-to-equity ratio

The debt-to-equity ratio is a financial ratio indicating the relative proportion of shareholders' equity and debt used to finance a company's assets. Closely related to leveraging, the ratio is also known as Risk, Gearing or Leverage. The two components are often taken from the firm's balance sheet or statement of financial position (so-called book value), but the ratio may also be calculated using market values for both, if the company's debt and equity are publicly traded, or using a combination of book value for debt and market value for equity financially.

Gross profit

In accounting, gross profit or sales profit is the difference between revenue and the cost of making a product or providing a service, before deducting overhead, payroll, taxation, and interest payments. Note that this is different from operating profit (earnings before interest and taxes).

The various deductions (and their corresponding metrics) leading from Net sales to Net income are as follow:Net sales = Gross sales - (Customer Discounts, Returns, Allowances)Gross profit = Net sales - Cost of goods soldOperating Profit = Gross Profit - Total operating expensesNet income (or Net profit) = Operating Profit - taxes - interest

(Note: cost of goods sold is calculated differently for a merchandising business than for a manufacturer).

Accounting profit

Accounting profit is the difference between price and the costs of bringing to market whatever it is that is accounted as an enterprise (whether by harvest, extraction, manufacture) in terms of the component costs of delivered goods and/or services and any operating or other expenses.

A key difficulty in measuring profit is in defining costs. Pure economic monetary profits can be zero or negative even in competitive equilibrium when accounted monetized costs exceed monetized price.

Operating margin

In business, operating margin - also known as operating income margin, operating profit margin and return on sales (ROS) - is the ratio of operating income ('operating profit' in the UK) divided by net sales, usually presented in percent.

$$\text{Operating margin} = \left(\frac{\text{Operating income}}{\text{Revenue}}\right)$$

Net profit measures the profitability of ventures after accounting for all costs.

Return on sales (ROS) is net profit as a percentage of sales revenue.

Net profit

Net profit, also referred to as the bottom line, net income, or net earnings is a measure of the profitability of a venture after accounting for all costs. In a survey of nearly 200 senior marketing managers, 91 percent responded that they found the 'net profit' metric very useful. In accounting, net profit is equal to the gross profit minus overheads minus interest payable for a given time period (usually: accounting period).

Net profit margin

Profit margin, net margin, net profit margin or net profit ratio all refer to a measure of profitability. It is calculated by finding the net profit as a percentage of the revenue.

3. Financial Statements and Ratio Analysis

CHAPTER HIGHLIGHTS & NOTES: KEY TERMS, PEOPLE, PLACES, CONCEPTS

$$\text{Net profit Margin} = \frac{\text{Net Profit}}{\text{Revenue}}$$ where Net Profit = Revenue - Cost

profit percentage is calculated with cost price taken as base.

Return on equity

Return on equity measures the rate of return on the ownership interest (shareholders' equity) of the common stock owners. It measures a firm's efficiency at generating profits from every unit of shareholders' equity (also known as net assets or assets minus liabilities). Return on equity shows how well a company uses investment funds to generate earnings growth.

CHAPTER QUIZ: KEY TERMS, PEOPLE, PLACES, CONCEPTS

1. _________ is a financial ratio that indicates the percentage of a company's assets that are provided via debt. It is the ratio of total debt (the sum of current liabilities and long-term liabilities) and total assets (the sum of current assets, fixed assets, and other assets such as 'goodwill').

$$\text{Debt ratio} = \frac{\text{Total Debt}}{\text{Total Assets}}$$

or alternatively:

$$\text{Debt ratio} = \frac{\text{Total Liability}}{\text{Total Assets}}$$

For example, a company with $2 million in total assets and $500,000 in total liabilities would have a _________ of 25%.

a. Debt ratio
b. Debt-to-capital ratio
c. Debt-to-equity ratio
d. Debt-to-GDP ratio

2. . A _________ is a formal record of the financial activities of a business, person, or other entity.

Relevant financial information is presented in a structured manner and in a form easy to understand.

They typically include basic _________s, accompanied by a management discussion and analysis:•Statement of financial position: also referred to as a balance sheet, reports on a company's assets, liabilities, and ownership equity at a given point in time.•Statement of comprehensive income: reports on a company's income, expenses, and profits over a period of time.

a. PnL Explained
b. Financial statement
c. Consolidated financial statement
d. Financial statement

3. _________, also called offer price, offer, asking price, or simply ask, is the price a seller states she or he will accept for a good.

The seller may qualify the stated asking price as firm or negotiable. Firm means the seller is saying he or she won't change the price.

a. Ask price
b. Earnings per share
c. Eurodollar
d. Income tax audit

4. (_________ or Contributed capital) refers to capital contributed to a corporation by investors through purchase of stock from the corporation (not through purchase of stock in the open market from other stockholders (secondary market)). It includes share capital (i.e. capital stock) as well as additional _________.

The _________ account does not reflect the amount of capital contributed by any specific investor.

a. Paid-in Capital
b. Earnings per share
c. Eurodollar
d. Income tax audit

5. The _________ is a private, not-for-profit organization whose primary purpose is to develop generally accepted accounting principles (GAAP) within the United States in the public's interest. The Securities and Exchange Commission (SEC) designated the _________ as the organization responsible for setting accounting standards for public companies in the U.S. It was created in 1973, replacing the Committee on Accounting Procedure (CAP) and the Accounting Principles Board (APB) of the American Institute of Certified Public Accountants (AICPA).

a. granularity
b. Jimmy Carter
c. Financial Accounting Standards Board
d. Gramm-Leach-Bliley Act

ANSWER KEY
3. Financial Statements and Ratio Analysis

---

1. a
2. b
3. a
4. a
5. c

You can take the complete Chapter Practice Test

for 3. Financial Statements and Ratio Analysis
on all key terms, persons, places, and concepts.

Online 99 Cents

http://www.JustTheFacts101.com

Use www.JustTheFacts101.com for all your study needs

including Facts101's online interactive problem solving labs in

chemistry, statistics, mathematics, and more.

4. Cash Flow and Financial Planning

CHAPTER OUTLINE: KEY TERMS, PEOPLE, PLACES, CONCEPTS

_______________ Cash flow

_______________ Financial planning

_______________ Ask price

_______________ Depreciation

_______________ Operating cash flow

_______________ Accounting profit

_______________ Free cash flow

_______________ Personal budget

_______________ Financial statement

_______________ External financing

CHAPTER HIGHLIGHTS & NOTES: KEY TERMS, PEOPLE, PLACES, CONCEPTS

Cash flow	Cash flow is the movement of money into or out of a business, project, or financial product. It is usually measured during a specified, limited period of time. Measurement of cash flow can be used for calculating other parameters that give information on a company's value and situation.
Financial planning	Financial planning is the task of determining how a business will afford to achieve its strategic goals and objectives. Usually, a company creates a Financial Plan immediately after the vision and objectives have been set. The Financial Plan describes each of the activities, resources, equipment and materials that are needed to achieve these objectives, as well as the timeframes involved.
Ask price	Ask price, also called offer price, offer, asking price, or simply ask, is the price a seller states she or he will accept for a good. The seller may qualify the stated asking price as firm or negotiable. Firm means the seller is saying he or she won't change the price.

Depreciation	In accountancy, depreciation refers to two aspects of the same concept:•the decrease in value of assets (fair value depreciation), and•the allocation of the cost of assets to periods in which the assets are used (depreciation with the matching principle). The former affects the balance sheet of a business or entity, and the latter affects the net income that they report. Generally the cost is allocated, as depreciation expense, among the periods in which the asset is expected to be used. This expense is recognized by businesses for financial reporting and tax purposes.
Operating cash flow	In financial accounting, operating cash flow, cash flow provided by operations or cash flow from operating activities (CFO), refers to the amount of cash a company generates from the revenues it brings in, excluding costs associated with long-term investment on capital items or investment in securities. The International Financial Reporting Standards defines operating cash flow as cash generated from operations less taxation and interest paid, investment income received and less dividends paid gives rise to operating cash flows. To calculate cash generated from operations, one must calculate cash generated from customers and cash paid to suppliers.
Accounting profit	Accounting profit is the difference between price and the costs of bringing to market whatever it is that is accounted as an enterprise (whether by harvest, extraction, manufacture) in terms of the component costs of delivered goods and/or services and any operating or other expenses. A key difficulty in measuring profit is in defining costs. Pure economic monetary profits can be zero or negative even in competitive equilibrium when accounted monetized costs exceed monetized price.
Free cash flow	In corporate finance, free cash flow is cash flow available for distribution among all the securities holders of a corporate entity. They include equity holders, debt holders, preferred stock holders, convertible security holders, and so on. Note that the first three lines above are calculated for you on the standard Statement of Cash Flows.
Personal budget	A family budget is a finance plan that allocates future personal income towards expenses, savings and debt repayment. Past spending and personal debt are considered when creating a personal budget. There are several methods and tools available for creating, using and adjusting a personal budget.
Financial statement	A financial statement is a formal record of the financial activities of a business, person, or other entity. Relevant financial information is presented in a structured manner and in a form easy to understand.

4. Cash Flow and Financial Planning

CHAPTER HIGHLIGHTS & NOTES: KEY TERMS, PEOPLE, PLACES, CONCEPTS

External financing	In the theory of capital structure, External financing is the phrase used to describe funds that firms obtain from outside of the firm. It is contrasted to internal financing which consists mainly of profits retained by the firm for investment. There are many kinds of external financing.

CHAPTER QUIZ: KEY TERMS, PEOPLE, PLACES, CONCEPTS

1. _________ is the task of determining how a business will afford to achieve its strategic goals and objectives. Usually, a company creates a Financial Plan immediately after the vision and objectives have been set. The Financial Plan describes each of the activities, resources, equipment and materials that are needed to achieve these objectives, as well as the timeframes involved.

   a. Financial planning
   b. Float
   c. Front-end loading
   d. Gantt chart

2. _________ is the movement of money into or out of a business, project, or financial product. It is usually measured during a specified, limited period of time. Measurement of _________ can be used for calculating other parameters that give information on a company's value and situation.

   a. Cash flow
   b. Cash flow statement
   c. Checkoff
   d. Clean surplus accounting

3. _________ is the difference between price and the costs of bringing to market whatever it is that is accounted as an enterprise (whether by harvest, extraction, manufacture) in terms of the component costs of delivered goods and/or services and any operating or other expenses.

   A key difficulty in measuring profit is in defining costs. Pure economic monetary profits can be zero or negative even in competitive equilibrium when accounted monetized costs exceed monetized price.

   a. Accounting profit
   b. Cash flow hedge
   c. Cash flow loan
   d. Discounted cash flow

4. _________, also called offer price, offer, asking price, or simply ask, is the price a seller states she or he will accept for a good.

The seller may qualify the stated asking price as firm or negotiable. Firm means the seller is saying he or she won't change the price.

a. Ask price
b. Earnings per share
c. Eurodollar
d. Income tax audit

5. In accountancy, _________ refers to two aspects of the same concept:•the decrease in value of assets (fair value _________), and•the allocation of the cost of assets to periods in which the assets are used (_________ with the matching principle).

The former affects the balance sheet of a business or entity, and the latter affects the net income that they report. Generally the cost is allocated, as _________ expense, among the periods in which the asset is expected to be used. This expense is recognized by businesses for financial reporting and tax purposes.

a. Detailed division of labor
b. Disability insurance
c. Depreciation
d. Discouraged worker

ANSWER KEY
4. Cash Flow and Financial Planning

---

1. a
2. a
3. a
4. a
5. c

You can take the complete Chapter Practice Test

for 4. Cash Flow and Financial Planning
on all key terms, persons, places, and concepts.

Online 99 Cents

http://www.JustTheFacts101.com

Use www.JustTheFacts101.com for all your study needs

including Facts101's online interactive problem solving labs in

chemistry, statistics, mathematics, and more.

5. Time Value of Money

CHAPTER OUTLINE: KEY TERMS, PEOPLE, PLACES, CONCEPTS

- Future value
- Business ethics
- Present value
- Annuity
- Principal
- Discounted cash flow
- Discounting
- Perpetuity
- Annual percentage rate
- Annual percentage yield

CHAPTER HIGHLIGHTS & NOTES: KEY TERMS, PEOPLE, PLACES, CONCEPTS

Future value	Future value is the value of an asset at a specific date. It measures the nominal future sum of money that a given sum of money is 'worth' at a specified time in the future assuming a certain interest rate, or more generally, rate of return; it is the present value multiplied by the accumulation function. The value does not include corrections for inflation or other factors that affect the true value of money in the future.
Business ethics	Business ethics is a form of applied ethics or professional ethics that examines ethical principles and moral or ethical problems that arise in a business environment. It applies to all aspects of business conduct and is relevant to the conduct of individuals and entire organizations. Business ethics has both normative and descriptive dimensions.
Present value	Present value, also known as present discounted value, is a future amount of money that has been discounted to reflect its current value, as if it existed today.

	The present value is always less than or equal to the future value because money has interest-earning potential, a characteristic referred to as the time value of money. Time value can be described with the simplified phrase, "A dollar today is worth more than a dollar tomorrow".
Annuity	The term annuity is used in finance theory, this is to refer to any terminating stream of fixed payments over a specified period of time. This usage is most commonly seen in discussions of finance, usually in connection with the valuation of the stream of payments, taking into account time value of money, concepts such as interest rate and future value. Examples of annuities are regular deposits to a savings account, monthly home mortgage payments and monthly insurance payments.
Principal	In commercial law, a principal is a person, legal or natural, who authorizes an agent to act to create one or more legal relationships with a third party. This branch of law is called agency and relies on the common law proposition qui facit per alium, facit per se . It is a parallel concept to vicarious liability and strict liability (in which one person is held liable for the acts or omissions of another) in criminal law or torts.
Discounted cash flow	In finance, discounted cash flow analysis is a method of valuing a project, company, or asset using the concepts of the time value of money. All future cash flows are estimated and discounted to give their present values (PVs)--the sum of all future cash flows, both incoming and outgoing, is the net present value (NPV), which is taken as the value or price of the cash flows in question. Present value may also be expressed as a number of years' purchase of the future undiscounted annual cash flows expected to arise.
Discounting	Discounting is a financial mechanism in which a debtor obtains the right to delay payments to a creditor, for a defined period of time, in exchange for a charge or fee. Essentially, the party that owes money in the present purchases the right to delay the payment until some future date. The discount, or charge, is simply the difference between the original amount owed in the present and the amount that has to be paid in the future to settle the debt.
Perpetuity	A perpetuity is an annuity that has no end, or a stream of cash payments that continues forever. There are few actual perpetuities in existence (the United Kingdom (UK) government has issued them in the past; these are known and still trade as consols). Real estate and preferred stock are among some types of investments that effect the results of a perpetuity, and prices can be established using techniques for valuing a perpetuity.
Annual percentage rate	The term annual percentage rate, also called nominal Annual percentage rate, and the term effective Annual percentage rate, also called EAPR, describes the interest rate for a whole year (annualized), rather than just a monthly fee/rate, as applied on a loan, mortgage loan, credit card, etc. It is a finance charge expressed as an annual rate.

5. Time Value of Money

CHAPTER HIGHLIGHTS & NOTES: KEY TERMS, PEOPLE, PLACES, CONCEPTS

Those terms have formal, legal definitions in some countries or legal jurisdictions, but in general:•The nominal Annual percentage rate is the simple-interest rate (for a year).•The effective Annual percentage rate is the fee+compound interest rate (calculated across a year).

The nominal Annual percentage rate is calculated as: the rate, for a payment period, multiplied by the number of payment periods in a year.

Annual percentage yield	Annual percentage yield (also called Effective Annual Rate (EAR) in finance) is a normalized representation of an interest rate, based on a compounding period of one year. Annual percentage yield figures allow for a reasonable, single-point comparison of different offerings with varying compounding schedules. However, it does not account for the possibility of account fees affecting the net gain.

CHAPTER QUIZ: KEY TERMS, PEOPLE, PLACES, CONCEPTS

1. In finance, _________ analysis is a method of valuing a project, company, or asset using the concepts of the time value of money. All future cash flows are estimated and discounted to give their present values (PVs)--the sum of all future cash flows, both incoming and outgoing, is the net present value (NPV), which is taken as the value or price of the cash flows in question. Present value may also be expressed as a number of years' purchase of the future undiscounted annual cash flows expected to arise.

   a. Discounted cash flow
   b. First Chicago Method
   c. Forecast period
   d. Free cash flow

2. _________ is the value of an asset at a specific date. It measures the nominal future sum of money that a given sum of money is 'worth' at a specified time in the future assuming a certain interest rate, or more generally, rate of return; it is the present value multiplied by the accumulation function. The value does not include corrections for inflation or other factors that affect the true value of money in the future.

   a. Graham number
   b. Heston model
   c. Future value
   d. Holding period return

3. . _________ is a form of applied ethics or professional ethics that examines ethical principles and moral or ethical problems that arise in a business environment. It applies to all aspects of business conduct and is relevant to the conduct of individuals and entire organizations.

_________ has both normative and descriptive dimensions.

a. Hypernorms
b. Business ethics
c. Corporate Knights
d. Jewish business ethics

4. _________, also known as present discounted value, is a future amount of money that has been discounted to reflect its current value, as if it existed today. The _________ is always less than or equal to the future value because money has interest-earning potential, a characteristic referred to as the time value of money. Time value can be described with the simplified phrase, "A dollar today is worth more than a dollar tomorrow".

a. Put-call parity
b. Present value
c. QuantLib
d. Range accrual

5. The term _________ is used in finance theory, this is to refer to any terminating stream of fixed payments over a specified period of time. This usage is most commonly seen in discussions of finance, usually in connection with the valuation of the stream of payments, taking into account time value of money, concepts such as interest rate and future value.

Examples of _________(ies) are regular deposits to a savings account, monthly home mortgage payments and monthly insurance payments.

a. Efficiency Based Absorption Costing
b. Annuity
c. QuantLib
d. Range accrual

ANSWER KEY
5. Time Value of Money

---

1. a
2. c
3. b
4. b
5. b

You can take the complete Chapter Practice Test

for 5. Time Value of Money
on all key terms, persons, places, and concepts.

Online 99 Cents

http://www.JustTheFacts101.com

Use www.JustTheFacts101.com for all your study needs

including Facts101's online interactive problem solving labs in

chemistry, statistics, mathematics, and more.

6. Interest Rates and Bond Valuation

CHAPTER OUTLINE: KEY TERMS, PEOPLE, PLACES, CONCEPTS

- Interest rate
- Liquidity preference
- Asset
- Deflation
- Term structure
- Flat yield
- Yield to maturity
- Market segmentation
- Risk premium
- Corporate bond
- Restrictive covenant
- Subordination
- Current yield
- Bond credit rating
- Moody's Investors Service
- Mortgage-backed security
- Eurobond
- Debenture
- Equipment trust certificate
- Mortgage bond
- Trust certificate

6. Interest Rates and Bond Valuation

CHAPTER OUTLINE: KEY TERMS, PEOPLE, PLACES, CONCEPTS

_______________ Valuation

_______________ Valuation risk

_______________ Cash flow

_______________ Business ethics

_______________ Premium Bond

_______________ Interest rate risk

CHAPTER HIGHLIGHTS & NOTES: KEY TERMS, PEOPLE, PLACES, CONCEPTS

Interest rate

An interest rate is the rate at which interest is paid by borrowers for the use of money that they borrow from a lender. Specifically, the interest rate is a percent of principal (P) paid a certain amount of times (m) per period (usually quoted per annum). For example, a small company borrows capital from a bank to buy new assets for its business, and in return the lender receives interest at a predetermined interest rate for deferring the use of funds and instead lending it to the borrower.

Liquidity preference

In macroeconomic theory, liquidity preference refers to the demand for money, considered as liquidity. The concept was first developed by John Maynard Keynes in his book The General Theory of Employment, Interest and Money (1936) to explain determination of the interest rate by the supply and demand for money.

Asset

In financial accounting, assets are economic resources. Anything tangible or intangible that is capable of being owned or controlled to produce value and that is held to have positive economic value is considered an asset. Simply stated, assets represent value of ownership that can be converted into cash (although cash itself is also considered an asset).

Deflation

In economics, deflation is a decrease in the general price level of goods and services. Deflation occurs when the inflation rate falls below 0% (a negative inflation rate). This should not be confused with disinflation, a slow-down in the inflation rate (i.e., when inflation declines to lower levels).

6. Interest Rates and Bond Valuation

CHAPTER HIGHLIGHTS & NOTES: KEY TERMS, PEOPLE, PLACES, CONCEPTS

Term structure

In finance, the yield curve is a curve showing several yields or interest rates across different contract lengths for a similar debt contract. The curve shows the relation between the (level of) interest rate (or cost of borrowing) and the time to maturity, known as the 'term', of the debt for a given borrower in a given currency. For example, the U.S. dollar interest rates paid on U.S. Treasury securities for various maturities are closely watched by many traders, and are commonly plotted on a graph such as the one on the right which is informally called 'the yield curve.' More formal mathematical descriptions of this relation are often called the term structure of interest rates.

Flat yield

The current yield, interest yield, income yield, flat yield, market yield, mark to market yield or running yield is a financial term used in reference to bonds and other fixed-interest securities such as gilts. It is the ratio of the annual interest payment and the bond's current clean price:

$$\text{Current yield} = \frac{\text{Annual interest payment}}{\text{Clean price}}.$$

The current yield only therefore refers to the yield of the bond at the current moment. It does not reflect the total return over the life of the bond.

Yield to maturity

The Yield to maturity, book yield or redemption yield of a bond or other fixed-interest security, such as gilts, is the internal rate of return (IRR, overall interest rate) earned by an investor who buys the bond today at the market price, assuming that the bond will be held until maturity, and that all coupon and principal payments will be made on schedule. Yield to maturity is simply the discount rate at which the sum of all future cash flows from the bond (coupons and principal) is equal to the price of the bond. The Yield to maturity is often given in terms of Annual Percentage Rate (A.P.R)., but more usually market convention is followed: in a number of major markets the convention is to quote yields semi-annually .

Market segmentation

Market segmentation is a marketing strategy that involves dividing a broad target market into subsets of consumers who have common needs, and then designing and implementing strategies to target their needs and desires using media channels and other touch-points that best allow to reach them.

Risk premium

Risk premium is the minimum amount of money by which the expected return on a risky asset must exceed the known return on a risk-free asset, or the expected return on a less risky asset, in order to induce an individual to hold the risky asset rather than the risk-free asset. (Note that risk premia may be negative). Thus it is the minimum willingness to accept compensation for the risk.

Corporate bond

A corporate bond is a bond issue by a corporation. It is a bond that a corporation issues to raise money effectively in order to expand its business. The term is usually applied to longer-term debt instruments, generally with a maturity date falling at least a year after their issue date.

Restrictive covenant

A restrictive covenant is a type of real covenant, a legal obligation imposed in a deed by the seller upon the buyer of real estate to do or not to do something. Such restrictions frequently 'run with the land' and are enforceable on subsequent buyers of the property. In jurisdictions that use the Torrens system of land registration, restrictive covenants are generally registered against title.

Subordination

Subordination in banking and finance refers to the order of priorities in claims for ownership or interest in various assets. Subordination of debt

Subordination is the process by which a creditor is placed in a lower priority for the collection of its debt from its debtor's assets than the priority the creditor previously had, In common parlance, the debt is said to be subordinated but in reality, it is the right of the creditor to collect the debt that has been reduced in priority. The priority of right to collect the debt is important when a debtor owes more than one creditor but has assets of insufficient value to pay them all in full at the time of a default.

Current yield

The current yield, interest yield, income yield, flat yield, market yield, mark to market yield or running yield is a financial term used in reference to bonds and other fixed-interest securities such as gilts. It is the ratio of the annual interest payment and the bond's current clean price:

$$\text{Current yield} = \frac{\text{Annual interest payment}}{\text{Clean price}}.$$

The current yield only therefore refers to the yield of the bond at the current moment. It does not reflect the total return over the life of the bond.

Bond credit rating

In investment, the bond credit rating assesses the credit worthiness of a corporation's or government debt issues. It is analogous to credit ratings for individuals.

The credit rating is a financial indicator to potential investors of debt securities such as bonds. These are assigned by credit rating agencies such as Moody's, Standard & Poor's, and Fitch Ratings to have letter designations (such as AAA, B, CC) which represent the quality of a bond. Bond ratings below BBB-/Baa are considered to be not investment grade and are colloquially called junk bonds.

Moody's Investors Service

Moody's Investors Service, is the bond credit rating business of Moody's Corporation, representing the company's traditional line of business and its historical name. Moody's Investors Service provides international financial research on bonds issued by commercial and government entities and, with Standard & Poor's and Fitch Group, is considered one of the Big Three credit rating agencies.

6. Interest Rates and Bond Valuation

CHAPTER HIGHLIGHTS & NOTES: KEY TERMS, PEOPLE, PLACES, CONCEPTS

Mortgage-backed security

A mortgage-backed security is a type of asset-backed security that is secured by a mortgage, or more commonly a collection ('pool') of sometimes hundreds of mortgages. The mortgages are sold to a financial institution (a government agency or investment bank) that 'securitizes', or packages, the loans together into a security that can be sold to investors. The mortgages of a Mortgage backed security may be residential or commercial; in the United States they may issued by structures set up by government-sponsored enterprises like Fannie Mae or Freddie Mac, or they can be 'private-label', issued by structures set up by investment banks.

Eurobond

A Eurobond is an international bond that is denominated in a currency not native to the country where it is issued. Also called external bond; 'external bonds which, strictly, are neither Eurobonds nor foreign bonds would also include: foreign currency denominated domestic bonds.

Debenture

A debenture is a document that either creates a debt or acknowledges it, and it is a debt without collateral. In corporate finance, the term is used for a medium- to long-term debt instrument used by large companies to borrow money. In some countries the term is used interchangeably with bond, loan stock or note.

Equipment trust certificate

An equipment trust certificate is a financial security used in aircraft finance, most commonly to take advantage of tax benefits in North America.

In a typical Equipment trust certificate transaction, a 'trust certificate' is sold to investors in order to finance the purchase of an aircraft by a trust managed on the investors' behalf. The trust then leases the aircraft to an airline, and the trustee routes payments through the trust to the investors. Upon maturity of the note, the airline receives title to the aircraft.

Mortgage bond

A mortgage bond is a bond backed by a pool of mortgages on a real estate asset such as a house. More generally, bonds which are secured by the pledge of specific assets are called mortgage bonds. Mortgage bonds can pay interest in either monthly, quarterly or semiannual periods.

Trust certificate

In finance, a trust certificate is a corporate bond backed by other securities, usually a parent corporation borrowing against securities of its subsidiaries.

Valuation

In finance, valuation is the process of estimating what something is worth. Items that are usually valued are a financial asset or liability. Valuations can be done on assets (for example, investments in marketable securities such as stocks, options, business enterprises, or intangible assets such as patents and trademarks) or on liabilities (e.g., bonds issued by a company).

Valuation risk

Valuation Risk is the financial risk that an asset is overvalued and is worth less than expected when it matures or is sold. Factors contributing to valuation risk can include incomplete data, market instability, financial modeling uncertainties and poor data analysis by the people responsible for determining the value of the asset. This risk can be a concern for investors, lenders, financial regulators and other people involved in the financial markets.

6. Interest Rates and Bond Valuation

CHAPTER HIGHLIGHTS & NOTES: KEY TERMS, PEOPLE, PLACES, CONCEPTS

Cash flow	Cash flow is the movement of money into or out of a business, project, or financial product. It is usually measured during a specified, limited period of time. Measurement of cash flow can be used for calculating other parameters that give information on a company's value and situation.
Business ethics	Business ethics is a form of applied ethics or professional ethics that examines ethical principles and moral or ethical problems that arise in a business environment. It applies to all aspects of business conduct and is relevant to the conduct of individuals and entire organizations. Business ethics has both normative and descriptive dimensions.
Premium Bond	A Premium Bond is a lottery bond issued by the United Kingdom government's National Savings and Investments agency. The bonds are entered in a regular prize draw and the government promises to buy them back, on request, for their original price. The bonds were introduced by Harold Macmillan in his 1956 budget.
Interest rate risk	Interest rate risk is the risk that arises for bond owners from fluctuating interest rates. How much interest rate risk a bond has depends on how sensitive its price is to interest rate changes in the market. The sensitivity depends on two things, the bond's time to maturity, and the coupon rate of the bond.

CHAPTER QUIZ: KEY TERMS, PEOPLE, PLACES, CONCEPTS

1. An _________ is the rate at which interest is paid by borrowers for the use of money that they borrow from a lender. Specifically, the _________ is a percent of principal (P) paid a certain amount of times (m) per period (usually quoted per annum). For example, a small company borrows capital from a bank to buy new assets for its business, and in return the lender receives interest at a predetermined _________ for deferring the use of funds and instead lending it to the borrower.

   a. Inverse demand function
   b. ExMark
   c. Optimal stopping
   d. Interest rate

2. . In economics, _________ is a decrease in the general price level of goods and services. _________ occurs when the inflation rate falls below 0% (a negative inflation rate). This should not be confused with disinflation, a slow-down in the inflation rate (i.e., when inflation declines to lower levels).

   a. Deflation
   b. Hyperinflation
   c. Monetary inflation

3. In financial accounting, _________s are economic resources. Anything tangible or intangible that is capable of being owned or controlled to produce value and that is held to have positive economic value is considered an _________. Simply stated, _________s represent value of ownership that can be converted into cash (although cash itself is also considered an _________).

   a. Accelerated depreciation
   b. Account
   c. Asset
   d. Accounts payable

4. In macroeconomic theory, _________ refers to the demand for money, considered as liquidity. The concept was first developed by John Maynard Keynes in his book The General Theory of Employment, Interest and Money (1936) to explain determination of the interest rate by the supply and demand for money.

   a. Medicon Valley
   b. Micro venture capital
   c. Midas List
   d. Liquidity preference

5. A _________ is a type of real covenant, a legal obligation imposed in a deed by the seller upon the buyer of real estate to do or not to do something. Such restrictions frequently 'run with the land' and are enforceable on subsequent buyers of the property. In jurisdictions that use the Torrens system of land registration, _________s are generally registered against title.

   a. Slumlord
   b. Restrictive covenant
   c. Supermarket shortage
   d. granularity

ANSWER KEY
6. Interest Rates and Bond Valuation

---

1. d

2. a

3. c

4. d

5. b

You can take the complete Chapter Practice Test

for 6. Interest Rates and Bond Valuation
on all key terms, persons, places, and concepts.

Online 99 Cents

http://www.JustTheFacts101.com

Use www.JustTheFacts101.com for all your study needs including Facts101's online interactive problem solving labs in chemistry, statistics, mathematics, and more.

7. Stock Valuation

CHAPTER OUTLINE: KEY TERMS, PEOPLE, PLACES, CONCEPTS

- Ask price
- Equity
- Common stock
- Preferred stock
- Par value
- Pre-emption right
- Treasury stock
- Issued shares
- Common stock dividend
- Proxy fight
- Proxy statement
- Dividend
- American depositary receipt
- American depositary share
- Venture capital
- Concept note
- Underwriting
- Valuation
- Efficient-market hypothesis
- Behavioral Finance
- Stock valuation

7. Stock Valuation

CHAPTER OUTLINE: KEY TERMS, PEOPLE, PLACES, CONCEPTS

_____ Cash flow

_____ Free cash flow

_____ Book value

_____ Liquidation

_____ Debt-to-equity ratio

_____ Capital asset

_____ Capital asset pricing model

_____ Capital budgeting

_____ Payback period

CHAPTER HIGHLIGHTS & NOTES: KEY TERMS, PEOPLE, PLACES, CONCEPTS

Ask price

Ask price, also called offer price, offer, asking price, or simply ask, is the price a seller states she or he will accept for a good.

The seller may qualify the stated asking price as firm or negotiable. Firm means the seller is saying he or she won't change the price.

Equity

Equity or Economic equality, is the concept or idea of fairness in economics, particularly as to taxation or welfare economics. More specifically it may refer to equal life chances regardless of identity, to provide all citizens with a basic and equal minimum of income/goods/services or to increase funds and commitment for redistribution.

Inequality and inequities have significantly increased in recent decades, possibly driven by the worldwide economic processes of globalisation, economic liberalisation and integration.

Common stock

Common stock is a form of corporate equity ownership, a type of security. The terms 'voting share' or 'ordinary share' are also used in other parts of the world; common stock being primarily used in the United States.

Preferred stock	Preferred stock is an equity security which may have any combination of features not possessed by common stock including properties of both an equity and a debt instruments, and is generally considered a hybrid instrument. Preferreds are senior (i.e. higher ranking) to common stock, but subordinate to bonds in terms of claim . Preferred stock usually carries no voting rights, but may carry a dividend and may have priority over common stock in the payment of dividends and upon liquidation.
Par value	Par value, in finance and accounting, means stated value or face value. From this come the expressions at par (at the par value), over par (over par value) and under par (under par value).
Pre-emption right	A pre-emption right, is a contractual right to acquire certain property newly coming into existence before it can be offered to any other person or entity. Also called a 'first option to buy.' It comes from the Latin verb emo, emere, emi, emptum, to buy or purchase, plus the inseparable preposition pre, before. A right to acquire existing property in preference to any other person is usually referred to as a right of first refusal.
Treasury stock	A treasury stock or reacquired stock is stock which is bought back by the issuing company, reducing the amount of outstanding stock on the open market . Stock repurchases are often used as a tax-efficient method to put cash into shareholders' hands, rather than paying dividends. Sometimes, companies do this when they feel that their stock is undervalued on the open market.
Issued shares	Issued shares is a term of law and finance for the quantity of shares of a corporation, which have been allocated and are subsequently held by shareholders. The act of creating new issued shares is called issuance, allocation or allotment. Allotment, in simplicity, is the creation of shares and their transfer to a subscriber.
Common stock dividend	A common stock dividend is the dividend paid to common stock owners from the profits of the company. Like other dividends, the payout is in the form of cash or other like stock. The law may regulate the size of the common stock dividend particularly when the payout is a cash distribution tantamount to a liquidation.
Proxy fight	A proxy fight is an event that may occur when a corporation's stockholders develop opposition to some aspect of the corporate governance, often focusing on directorial and management positions. Corporate activists may attempt to persuade shareholders to use their proxy votes (i.e. votes by one individual or institution as the authorized representative of another) to install new management for any of a variety of reasons. Shareholders of a public corporation may appoint an agent to attend shareholder meetings and vote on their behalf.
Proxy statement	A proxy statement is a statement required of a firm when soliciting shareholder votes.

	This statement is filed in advance of the annual meeting. The firm needs to file a proxy statement, otherwise known as a Form DEF 14A (Definitive Proxy Statement), with the U.S. Securities and Exchange Commission.
Dividend	A dividend is a payment made by a corporation to its shareholders, usually as a distribution of profits. When a corporation earns a profit or surplus, it can either re-invest it in the business (called retained earnings), or it can distribute it to shareholders. A corporation may retain a portion of its earnings and pay the remainder as a dividend.
American depositary receipt	An American depositary receipt is a negotiable security that represents securities of a non-US company that trades in the US financial markets. Securities of a foreign company that are represented by an American depositary receipt are called American depositary shares (ADSs). Shares of many non-US companies trade on US stock exchanges through American depositary receipts.
American depositary share	An American depositary share is a vehicle for foreign corporations to list their ordinary equity on an American stock exchange, such as the New York Stock Exchange or the NASDAQ. Foreign corporations listed in other markets are not permitted to make direct secondary listings in the United States markets, thus this form of indirect ownership has been devised. American depositary shares are US-dollar denominated and each share represents one or more underlying shares in the subject. These American depositary shares confer full rights of ownership (including dividends, voting rights) to these underlying shares, which are held on deposit by a custodian bank in the company's home country or territory.
Venture capital	Venture capital is financial capital provided to early-stage, high-potential, high risk, growth startup companies. The venture capital fund makes money by owning equity in the companies it invests in, which usually have a novel technology or business model in high technology industries, such as biotechnology, IT and software. The typical venture capital investment occurs after the seed funding round as growth funding round (also referred to as Series A round) in the interest of generating a return through an eventual realization event, such as an IPO or trade sale of the company.
Concept note	A concept note, also called a prospectus, is a preliminary description of the ideas behind a project. Businesses, academic programs, and nonprofit organizations use them to help test and refine concepts and to communicate about the project with potential readers, including partners and donors, supervisors, or review boards or committees.

Underwriting	Underwriting refers to the process that a large financial service provider uses to assess the eligibility of a customer to receive their products (equity capital, insurance, mortgage, or credit). The name derives from the Lloyd's of London insurance market. Financial bankers, who would accept some of the risk on a given venture (historically a sea voyage with associated risks of shipwreck) in exchange for a premium, would literally write their names under the risk information that was written on a Lloyd's slip created for this purpose.
Valuation	In finance, valuation is the process of estimating what something is worth. Items that are usually valued are a financial asset or liability. Valuations can be done on assets (for example, investments in marketable securities such as stocks, options, business enterprises, or intangible assets such as patents and trademarks) or on liabilities (e.g., bonds issued by a company).
Efficient-market hypothesis	In finance, the efficient-market hypothesis, or the Joint Hypothesis Problem, asserts that financial markets are 'informationally efficient'. In consequence of this, one cannot consistently achieve returns in excess of average market returns on a risk-adjusted basis, given the information available at the time the investment is made. There are three major versions of the hypothesis: 'weak', 'semi-strong', and 'strong'.
Behavioral Finance	Behavioral economics and the related field, behavioral finance, study the effects of social, cognitive, and emotional factors on the economic decisions of individuals and institutions and the consequences for market prices, returns, and the resource allocation. The fields are primarily concerned with the bounds of rationality of economic agents. Behavioral models typically integrate insights from psychology with neo-classical economic theory.
Stock valuation	In financial markets, stock valuation is the method of calculating theoretical values of companies and their stocks. The main use of these methods is to predict future market prices, or more generally, potential market prices, and thus to profit from price movement - stocks that are judged undervalued (with respect to their theoretical value) are bought, while stocks that are judged overvalued are sold, in the expectation that undervalued stocks will, on the whole, rise in value, while overvalued stocks will, on the whole, fall. In the view of fundamental analysis, stock valuation based on fundamentals aims to give an estimate of their intrinsic value of the stock, based on predictions of the future cash flows and profitability of the business.
Cash flow	Cash flow is the movement of money into or out of a business, project, or financial product. It is usually measured during a specified, limited period of time. Measurement of cash flow can be used for calculating other parameters that give information on a company's value and situation.
Free cash flow	In corporate finance, free cash flow is cash flow available for distribution among all the securities holders of a corporate entity.

They include equity holders, debt holders, preferred stock holders, convertible security holders, and so on.

Note that the first three lines above are calculated for you on the standard Statement of Cash Flows.

Book value

In accounting, book value or carrying value is the value of an asset according to its balance sheet account balance. For assets, the value is based on the original cost of the asset less any depreciation, amortization or impairment costs made against the asset. Traditionally, a company's book value is its total assets minus intangible assets and liabilities.

Liquidation

In law, liquidation is the process by which a company is brought to an end, and the assets and property of the company redistributed. Liquidation is also sometimes referred to as winding-up or dissolution, although dissolution technically refers to the last stage of liquidation. The process of liquidation also arises when customs, an authority or agency in a country responsible for collecting and safeguarding customs duties, determines the final computation or ascertainment of the duties or drawback accruing on an entry.

Debt-to-equity ratio

The debt-to-equity ratio is a financial ratio indicating the relative proportion of shareholders' equity and debt used to finance a company's assets. Closely related to leveraging, the ratio is also known as Risk, Gearing or Leverage. The two components are often taken from the firm's balance sheet or statement of financial position (so-called book value), but the ratio may also be calculated using market values for both, if the company's debt and equity are publicly traded, or using a combination of book value for debt and market value for equity financially.

Capital asset

The term capital asset has three vaguely related definitions in specific accounting regimes and theories of economics. It is also used to refer to assets, including investments not held for sale, conversion or consumption# in the ordinary course of work or production or business. In the context of the capital asset pricing model it refers strictly to financialized instruments.

Capital asset pricing model

In finance, the capital asset pricing model is used to determine a theoretically appropriate required rate of return of an asset, if that asset is to be added to an already well-diversified portfolio, given that asset's non-diversifiable risk. The model takes into account the asset's sensitivity to non-diversifiable risk (also known as systematic risk or market risk), often represented by the quantity beta (ß) in the financial industry, as well as the expected return of the market and the expected return of a theoretical risk-free asset. Capital asset pricing model “suggests that an investor's cost of equity capital is determined by beta.” An extension to the Capital asset pricing model is the dual-beta model, which differentiates downside beta from upside beta.

CHAPTER HIGHLIGHTS & NOTES: KEY TERMS, PEOPLE, PLACES, CONCEPTS

Capital budgeting	Capital budgeting is the planning process used to determine whether an organization's long term investments such as new machinery, replacement machinery, new plants, new products, and research development projects are worth the funding of cash through the firm's capitalization structure (debt, equity or retained earnings). It is the process of allocating resources for major capital, or investment, expenditures. One of the primary goals of capital budgeting investments is to increase the value of the firm to the shareholders.
Payback period	Payback period in capital budgeting refers to the period of time required for the return on an investment to 'repay' the sum of the original investment. For example, a $1000 investment which returned $500 per year would have a two year payback period. The time value of money is not taken into account.

CHAPTER QUIZ: KEY TERMS, PEOPLE, PLACES, CONCEPTS

1. An _________ is a negotiable security that represents securities of a non-US company that trades in the US financial markets. Securities of a foreign company that are represented by an _________ are called American depositary shares (ADSs).

   Shares of many non-US companies trade on US stock exchanges through _________s.

   a. At the opening
   b. American depositary receipt
   c. Employee stock option
   d. Egyptian Exchange

2. _________, also called offer price, offer, asking price, or simply ask, is the price a seller states she or he will accept for a good.

   The seller may qualify the stated asking price as firm or negotiable. Firm means the seller is saying he or she won't change the price.

   a. Ask price
   b. Earnings per share
   c. Eurodollar
   d. Income tax audit

3. . _________, in finance and accounting, means stated value or face value. From this come the expressions at par (at the _________), over par (over _________) and under par (under _________).

a. Participation certificate
b. Par value
c. Performance attribution
d. Periodic deposit

4. A _________ is a statement required of a firm when soliciting shareholder votes. This statement is filed in advance of the annual meeting. The firm needs to file a _________, otherwise known as a Form DEF 14A (Definitive _________), with the U.S. Securities and Exchange Commission.

a. Proxy statement
b. Schedule 13D
c. Schedule 13G
d. Schedule TO

5. _________ is a form of corporate equity ownership, a type of security. The terms 'voting share' or 'ordinary share' are also used in other parts of the world; _________ being primarily used in the United States.

It is called 'common' to distinguish it from preferred stock.

a. Common stock
b. Control premium
c. Corporate synergy
d. Critical accounting policy

ANSWER KEY
7. Stock Valuation

1. b
2. a
3. b
4. a
5. a

You can take the complete Chapter Practice Test

for 7. Stock Valuation
on all key terms, persons, places, and concepts.

Online 99 Cents

http://www.JustTheFacts101.com

Use www.JustTheFacts101.com for all your study needs

including Facts101's online interactive problem solving labs in

chemistry, statistics, mathematics, and more.

8. Risk and Return

CHAPTER OUTLINE: KEY TERMS, PEOPLE, PLACES, CONCEPTS

- Capital
- Capital asset
- Ponzi scheme
- P3M3
- Capital asset pricing model
- Common stock
- Risk aversion
- Risk neutral
- Risk assessment
- Scenario analysis
- Bar chart
- Dispersion
- Standard deviation
- Coefficient of variation
- Diversification
- Political risk
- Risk premium
- Asset
- Security market line

8. Risk and Return

CHAPTER HIGHLIGHTS & NOTES: KEY TERMS, PEOPLE, PLACES, CONCEPTS

Capital	In economics, capital, capital goods, or real capital are those already-produced durable goods that are used in production of goods or services. The capital goods are not significantly consumed, though they may depreciate in the production process. Capital is distinct from land in that capital must itself be produced by human labor before it can be a factor of production.
Capital asset	The term capital asset has three vaguely related definitions in specific accounting regimes and theories of economics. It is also used to refer to assets, including investments not held for sale, conversion or consumption# in the ordinary course of work or production or business. In the context of the capital asset pricing model it refers strictly to financialized instruments.
Ponzi scheme	A Ponzi scheme is a fraudulent investment operation that pays returns to its investors from their own money or the money paid by subsequent investors, rather than from profit earned by the individual or organization running the operation. The Ponzi scheme usually entices new investors by offering higher returns than other investments, in the form of short-term returns that are either abnormally high or unusually consistent. Perpetuation of the high returns requires an ever-increasing flow of money from new investors to keep the scheme going.
P3M3	P3M3, also known as the Portfolio, Programme and Project Management Maturity Model is a reference guide for structured best practice. It breaks down the broad disciplines of portfolio, programme and project management into a hierarchy of Key Process Areas (KPAs). The hierarchical approach enables organisations to assess their current capability and then plot a roadmap for improvement prioritised by those KPAs which will make the biggest impact on performance.
Capital asset pricing model	In finance, the capital asset pricing model is used to determine a theoretically appropriate required rate of return of an asset, if that asset is to be added to an already well-diversified portfolio, given that asset's non-diversifiable risk. The model takes into account the asset's sensitivity to non-diversifiable risk (also known as systematic risk or market risk), often represented by the quantity beta (ß) in the financial industry, as well as the expected return of the market and the expected return of a theoretical risk-free asset. Capital asset pricing model "suggests that an investor's cost of equity capital is determined by beta." An extension to the Capital asset pricing model is the dual-beta model, which differentiates downside beta from upside beta.
Common stock	Common stock is a form of corporate equity ownership, a type of security. The terms 'voting share' or 'ordinary share' are also used in other parts of the world; common stock being primarily used in the United States. It is called 'common' to distinguish it from preferred stock.
Risk aversion	Risk aversion is a concept in psychology, economics, and finance, based on the behavior of humans while exposed to uncertainty to attempt to reduce that uncertainty.

Risk aversion is the reluctance of a person to accept a bargain with an uncertain payoff rather than another bargain with a more certain, but possibly lower, expected payoff. For example, a risk-averse investor might choose to put his or her money into a bank account with a low but guaranteed interest rate, rather than into a stock that may have high expected returns, but also involves a chance of losing value.

Risk neutral

In economics and finance, risk neutral preferences are neither risk averse nor risk seeking. A risk neutral party's decisions are not affected by the degree of uncertainty in a set of outcomes, so a risk neutral party is indifferent between choices with equal expected payoffs even if one choice is riskier. For example, if offered either €50 or a 50% chance each of €100 and €0, a risk neutral person would have no preference.

Risk assessment

Risk assessment is the determination of quantitative or qualitative value of risk related to a concrete situation and a recognized threat . Quantitative risk assessment requires calculations of two components of risk (R):, the magnitude of the potential loss (L), and the probability (p) that the loss will occur. Acceptable risk is a risk that is understood and tolerated usually because the cost or difficulty of implementing an effective countermeasure for the associated vulnerability exceeds the expectation of loss.

Scenario analysis

Scenario analysis is a process of analyzing possible future events by considering alternative possible outcomes (sometimes called 'alternative worlds'). Thus, the scenario analysis, which is a main method of projections, does not try to show one exact picture of the future. Instead, it presents consciously several alternative future developments.

Bar chart

A bar chart is a chart with rectangular bars with lengths proportional to the values that they represent. The bars can be plotted vertically or horizontally. A vertical bar chart is sometimes called a column bar chart.

Dispersion

Dispersion is a measure for the statistical distribution of portfolio returns. It is the asset-weighted standard deviation of individual portfolio returns within a comparable client group (composite) from the composite return.

Dispersion is of the following types:

(i)Range

(ii)Variance

(iii)Standard Deviation

(iv)Mean Deviation

8. Risk and Return

CHAPTER HIGHLIGHTS & NOTES: KEY TERMS, PEOPLE, PLACES, CONCEPTS

Standard deviation	In statistics and probability theory, standard deviation shows how much variation or 'dispersion' exists from the average (mean, or expected value).A low standard deviation indicates that the data points tend to be very close to the mean.High standard deviation indicates that the data points are spread out over a large range of values. The standard deviation of a random variable, statistical population, data set, or probability distribution is the square root of its variance. It is algebraically simpler though practically less robust than the average absolute deviation.
Coefficient of variation	In probability theory and statistics, the coefficient of variation is a normalized measure of dispersion of a probability distribution. It is also known as unitized risk or the variation coefficient. The absolute value of the CV is sometimes known as relative standard deviation (RSD), which is expressed as a percentage. The coefficient of variation (CV) is defined as the ratio of the standard deviation σ to the mean μ: $c_v = \frac{\sigma}{\mu}$ which is the inverse of the signal-to-noise ratio. It shows the extent of variability in relation to mean of the population.
Diversification	Diversification is a form of corporate strategy for a company. It seeks to increase profitability through greater sales volume obtained from new products and new markets. Diversification can occur either at the business unit level or at the corporate level.
Political risk	Political risk is a type of risk faced by investors, corporations, and governments. It is a risk that can be understood and managed with reasoned foresight and investment. Broadly, political risk refers to the complications businesses and governments may face as a result of what are commonly referred to as political decisions--or "any political change that alters the expected outcome and value of a given economic action by changing the probability of achieving business objectives".
Risk premium	Risk premium is the minimum amount of money by which the expected return on a risky asset must exceed the known return on a risk-free asset, or the expected return on a less risky asset, in order to induce an individual to hold the risky asset rather than the risk-free asset. (Note that risk premia may be negative). Thus it is the minimum willingness to accept compensation for the risk.
Asset	In financial accounting, assets are economic resources. Anything tangible or intangible that is capable of being owned or controlled to produce value and that is held to have positive economic value is considered an asset.

CHAPTER HIGHLIGHTS & NOTES: KEY TERMS, PEOPLE, PLACES, CONCEPTS

Security market line	Security market line is the representation of the Capital asset pricing model. It displays the expected rate of return of an individual security as a function of systematic, non-diversifiable risk (its beta).

CHAPTER QUIZ: KEY TERMS, PEOPLE, PLACES, CONCEPTS

1. _________ is a form of corporate strategy for a company. It seeks to increase profitability through greater sales volume obtained from new products and new markets. _________ can occur either at the business unit level or at the corporate level.

   a. Diversity marketing
   b. Diversification
   c. Free gift
   d. Global marketing

2. In finance, the _________ is used to determine a theoretically appropriate required rate of return of an asset, if that asset is to be added to an already well-diversified portfolio, given that asset's non-diversifiable risk. The model takes into account the asset's sensitivity to non-diversifiable risk (also known as systematic risk or market risk), often represented by the quantity beta (ß) in the financial industry, as well as the expected return of the market and the expected return of a theoretical risk-free asset. _________ "suggests that an investor's cost of equity capital is determined by beta." An extension to the _________ is the dual-beta model, which differentiates downside beta from upside beta.

   a. Cash accumulation equation
   b. Chen model
   c. Capital asset pricing model
   d. Constant elasticity of variance model

3. _________ is a form of corporate equity ownership, a type of security. The terms 'voting share' or 'ordinary share' are also used in other parts of the world; _________ being primarily used in the United States.

   It is called 'common' to distinguish it from preferred stock.

   a. Common stock
   b. Control premium
   c. Corporate synergy
   d. Critical accounting policy

4. . _________ is the representation of the Capital asset pricing model. It displays the expected rate of return of an individual security as a function of systematic, non-diversifiable risk (its beta).

   a. Benchmark-driven investment strategy

b. Security market line
c. Binary option
d. Bond credit rating

5. A _________ is a fraudulent investment operation that pays returns to its investors from their own money or the money paid by subsequent investors, rather than from profit earned by the individual or organization running the operation. The _________ usually entices new investors by offering higher returns than other investments, in the form of short-term returns that are either abnormally high or unusually consistent. Perpetuation of the high returns requires an ever-increasing flow of money from new investors to keep the scheme going.

a. granularity
b. Commission
c. Ponzi scheme
d. Constant proportion portfolio insurance

ANSWER KEY
8. Risk and Return

1. b
2. c
3. a
4. b
5. c

You can take the complete Chapter Practice Test

for 8. Risk and Return
on all key terms, persons, places, and concepts.

Online 99 Cents

http://www.JustTheFacts101.com

Use www.JustTheFacts101.com for all your study needs

including Facts101's online interactive problem solving labs in

chemistry, statistics, mathematics, and more.

9. The Cost of Capital

CHAPTER OUTLINE: KEY TERMS, PEOPLE, PLACES, CONCEPTS

- Common stock
- Debt capital
- Preferred stock
- Capital
- Capital budgeting
- Annual percentage rate
- Dividend
- Valuation
- Capital asset
- Retained earnings
- Weighted average cost of capital
- Average cost
- Book value
- Capital market
- Market value
- Weight function

9. The Cost of Capital

CHAPTER HIGHLIGHTS & NOTES: KEY TERMS, PEOPLE, PLACES, CONCEPTS

Common stock	Common stock is a form of corporate equity ownership, a type of security. The terms 'voting share' or 'ordinary share' are also used in other parts of the world; common stock being primarily used in the United States. It is called 'common' to distinguish it from preferred stock.
Debt capital	Debt capital is the capital that a business raises by taking out a loan. It is a loan made to a company that is normally repaid at some future date. Debt capital differs from equity or share capital because subscribers to debt capital do not become part owners of the business, but are merely creditors, and the suppliers of debt capital usually receive a contractually fixed annual percentage return on their loan, and this is known as the coupon rate.
Preferred stock	Preferred stock is an equity security which may have any combination of features not possessed by common stock including properties of both an equity and a debt instruments, and is generally considered a hybrid instrument. Preferreds are senior (i.e. higher ranking) to common stock, but subordinate to bonds in terms of claim . Preferred stock usually carries no voting rights, but may carry a dividend and may have priority over common stock in the payment of dividends and upon liquidation.
Capital	In economics, capital, capital goods, or real capital are those already-produced durable goods that are used in production of goods or services. The capital goods are not significantly consumed, though they may depreciate in the production process. Capital is distinct from land in that capital must itself be produced by human labor before it can be a factor of production.
Capital budgeting	Capital budgeting is the planning process used to determine whether an organization's long term investments such as new machinery, replacement machinery, new plants, new products, and research development projects are worth the funding of cash through the firm's capitalization structure (debt, equity or retained earnings). It is the process of allocating resources for major capital, or investment, expenditures. One of the primary goals of capital budgeting investments is to increase the value of the firm to the shareholders.
Annual percentage rate	The term annual percentage rate, also called nominal Annual percentage rate, and the term effective Annual percentage rate, also called EAPR, describes the interest rate for a whole year (annualized), rather than just a monthly fee/rate, as applied on a loan, mortgage loan, credit card, etc. It is a finance charge expressed as an annual rate. Those terms have formal, legal definitions in some countries or legal jurisdictions, but in general:•The nominal Annual percentage rate is the simple-interest rate (for a year).•The effective Annual percentage rate is the fee+compound interest rate (calculated across a year).

Dividend	A dividend is a payment made by a corporation to its shareholders, usually as a distribution of profits. When a corporation earns a profit or surplus, it can either re-invest it in the business (called retained earnings), or it can distribute it to shareholders. A corporation may retain a portion of its earnings and pay the remainder as a dividend.
Valuation	In finance, valuation is the process of estimating what something is worth. Items that are usually valued are a financial asset or liability. Valuations can be done on assets (for example, investments in marketable securities such as stocks, options, business enterprises, or intangible assets such as patents and trademarks) or on liabilities (e.g., bonds issued by a company).
Capital asset	The term capital asset has three vaguely related definitions in specific accounting regimes and theories of economics. It is also used to refer to assets, including investments not held for sale, conversion or consumption# in the ordinary course of work or production or business. In the context of the capital asset pricing model it refers strictly to financialized instruments.
Retained earnings	In accounting, retained earnings refers to the portion of net income of a corporation that is retained by the corporation rather than distributed to shareholders as dividends, or as the amount available to the corporation for distribution to shareholders. Similarly, if the corporation incurs a loss, then that loss reduces the corporation's retained earnings balance. If the balance of the retained earnings account is negative it may be called retained losses, accumulated losses or accumulated deficit, or similar terminology.
Weighted average cost of capital	The weighted average cost of capital is the rate that a company is expected to pay on average to all its security holders to finance its assets. The WACC is the minimum return that a company must earn on an existing asset base to satisfy its creditors, owners, and other providers of capital, or they will invest elsewhere. Companies raise money from a number of sources: common equity, preferred stock, straight debt, convertible debt, exchangeable debt, warrants, options, pension liabilities, executive stock options, governmental subsidies, and so on.
Average cost	In economics, average cost is equal to total cost divided by the number of goods produced (the output quantity, Q). It is also equal to the sum of average variable costs (total variable costs divided by Q) plus average fixed costs (total fixed costs divided by Q). Average costs may be dependent on the time period considered (increasing production may be expensive or impossible in the short term, for example).
Book value	In accounting, book value or carrying value is the value of an asset according to its balance sheet account balance. For assets, the value is based on the original cost of the asset less any depreciation, amortization or impairment costs made against the asset. Traditionally, a company's book value is its total assets minus intangible assets and liabilities.

9. The Cost of Capital

CHAPTER HIGHLIGHTS & NOTES: KEY TERMS, PEOPLE, PLACES, CONCEPTS

Capital market	Capital markets are financial markets for the buying and selling of long-term debt- or equity-backed securities. These markets channel the wealth of savers to those who can put it to long-term productive use, such as companies or governments making long-term investments. Financial regulators, such as the UK's Bank of England (BoE) or the U.S. Securities and Exchange Commission (SEC), oversee the capital markets in their jurisdictions to protect investors against fraud, among other duties.
Market value	Market value is the price at which an asset would trade in a competitive auction setting. Market value is often used interchangeably with open market value, fair value or fair market value, although these terms have distinct definitions in different standards, and may differ in some circumstances.
Weight function	A weight function is a mathematical device used when performing a sum, integral, or average to give some elements more 'weight' or influence on the result than other elements in the same set. They occur frequently in statistics and analysis, and are closely related to the concept of a measure. Weight functions can be employed in both discrete and continuous settings.

CHAPTER QUIZ: KEY TERMS, PEOPLE, PLACES, CONCEPTS

1. The term _________, also called nominal _________, and the term effective _________, also called EAPR, describes the interest rate for a whole year (annualized), rather than just a monthly fee/rate, as applied on a loan, mortgage loan, credit card, etc. It is a finance charge expressed as an annual rate. Those terms have formal, legal definitions in some countries or legal jurisdictions, but in general:•The nominal _________ is the simple-interest rate (for a year).•The effective _________ is the fee+compound interest rate (calculated across a year).

   The nominal _________ is calculated as: the rate, for a payment period, multiplied by the number of payment periods in a year.

   a. Arrow-Debreu model
   b. AZFinText
   c. Annual percentage rate
   d. Enterprise value

2. . _________ is an equity security which may have any combination of features not possessed by common stock including properties of both an equity and a debt instruments, and is generally considered a hybrid instrument. Preferreds are senior (i.e. higher ranking) to common stock, but subordinate to bonds in terms of claim .

   _________ usually carries no voting rights, but may carry a dividend and may have priority over common stock in the payment of dividends and upon liquidation.

a. Private equity
b. Preferred stock
c. Public float
d. Public offering

3. The term _________ has three vaguely related definitions in specific accounting regimes and theories of economics. It is also used to refer to assets, including investments not held for sale, conversion or consumption# in the ordinary course of work or production or business. In the context of the _________ pricing model it refers strictly to financialized instruments.

a. Collateralized fund obligation
b. Commission
c. Conditional variance swap
d. Capital asset

4. In economics, _________ is equal to total cost divided by the number of goods produced (the output quantity, Q). It is also equal to the sum of average variable costs (total variable costs divided by Q) plus average fixed costs (total fixed costs divided by Q). _________s may be dependent on the time period considered (increasing production may be expensive or impossible in the short term, for example).

a. Average fixed cost
b. Average cost
c. Bank condition
d. Beta

5. _________ is a form of corporate equity ownership, a type of security. The terms 'voting share' or 'ordinary share' are also used in other parts of the world; _________ being primarily used in the United States.

It is called 'common' to distinguish it from preferred stock.

a. Conditional budgeting
b. Control premium
c. Corporate synergy
d. Common stock

ANSWER KEY
9. The Cost of Capital

---

1. c
2. b
3. d
4. b
5. d

You can take the complete Chapter Practice Test

for 9. The Cost of Capital

on all key terms, persons, places, and concepts.

Online 99 Cents

http://www.JustTheFacts101.com

Use www.JustTheFacts101.com for all your study needs

including Facts101's online interactive problem solving labs in

chemistry, statistics, mathematics, and more.

10. Capital Budgeting Techniques

CHAPTER OUTLINE: KEY TERMS, PEOPLE, PLACES, CONCEPTS

- Capital
- Capital budgeting
- Ask price
- Cost
- Process capital
- Mutually exclusive
- Payback period
- Personal finance
- Net present value
- Present value
- Business ethics
- Profitability index
- Economic value
- Economic Value Added
- Pure economic loss
- Internal rate of return
- Cash flow

Capital

In economics, capital, capital goods, or real capital are those already-produced durable goods that are used in production of goods or services. The capital goods are not significantly consumed, though they may depreciate in the production process. Capital is distinct from land in that capital must itself be produced by human labor before it can be a factor of production.

Capital budgeting

Capital budgeting is the planning process used to determine whether an organization's long term investments such as new machinery, replacement machinery, new plants, new products, and research development projects are worth the funding of cash through the firm's capitalization structure (debt, equity or retained earnings). It is the process of allocating resources for major capital, or investment, expenditures. One of the primary goals of capital budgeting investments is to increase the value of the firm to the shareholders.

Ask price

Ask price, also called offer price, offer, asking price, or simply ask, is the price a seller states she or he will accept for a good.

The seller may qualify the stated asking price as firm or negotiable. Firm means the seller is saying he or she won't change the price.

Cost

In production, research, retail, and accounting, a cost is the value of money that has been used up to produce something, and hence is not available for use anymore. In business, the cost may be one of acquisition, in which case the amount of money expended to acquire it is counted as cost. In this case, money is the input that is gone in order to acquire the thing.

Process capital

Process capital is the value to an enterprise which is derived from the techniques, procedures, and programs that implement and enhance the delivery of goods and services. Process capital is one of the three components of structural capital, itself a component of intellectual capital. Process capital can be seen as the value of processes to any entity, whether for profit or not-for profit, but is most commonly used in reference to for-profit entities.

Mutually exclusive

Two events are 'mutually exclusive' if they cannot occur at the same time. An example is tossing a coin once, which can result in either heads or tails, but not both.

In the coin-tossing example, both outcomes are collectively exhaustive, which means that at least one of the outcomes must happen, so these two possibilities together exhaust all the possibilities.

Payback period

Payback period in capital budgeting refers to the period of time required for the return on an investment to 'repay' the sum of the original investment. For example, a $1000 investment which returned $500 per year would have a two year payback period. The time value of money is not taken into account.

10. Capital Budgeting Techniques

CHAPTER HIGHLIGHTS & NOTES: KEY TERMS, PEOPLE, PLACES, CONCEPTS

Personal finance

Personal finance refers to the financial management of which an individual or a family unit is required to make to obtain, budget, save, and spend monetary resources over time, taking into account various financial risks and future life events. When planning personal finances the individual would consider the suitability to his or her needs of a range of banking products (checking, savings accounts, credit cards and consumer loans) or investment (stock market, bonds, mutual funds) and insurance (life insurance, health insurance, disability insurance) products or participation and monitoring of individual- or employer-sponsored retirement plans, social security benefits, and income tax management.

Net present value

In finance, the Net Present Value or Net Present Worth (NPW) of a time series of cash flows, both incoming and outgoing, is defined as the sum of the present values (PVs) of the individual cash flows of the same entity.

In the case when all future cash flows are incoming (such as coupons and principal of a bond) and the only outflow of cash is the purchase price, the Net present value is simply the PV of future cash flows minus the purchase price (which is its own PV). Net present value is a central tool in discounted cash flow (DCF) analysis and is a standard method for using the time value of money to appraise long-term projects.

Present value

Present value, also known as present discounted value, is a future amount of money that has been discounted to reflect its current value, as if it existed today. The present value is always less than or equal to the future value because money has interest-earning potential, a characteristic referred to as the time value of money. Time value can be described with the simplified phrase, "A dollar today is worth more than a dollar tomorrow".

Business ethics

Business ethics is a form of applied ethics or professional ethics that examines ethical principles and moral or ethical problems that arise in a business environment. It applies to all aspects of business conduct and is relevant to the conduct of individuals and entire organizations.

Business ethics has both normative and descriptive dimensions.

Profitability index

Profitability index, also known as profit investment ratio (PIR) and value investment ratio (VIR), is the ratio of payoff to investment of a proposed project. It is a useful tool for ranking projects because it allows you to quantify the amount of value created per unit of investment.

The ratio is calculated as follows:•

$$\text{Profitability index} = \frac{\text{PV of future cash flows}}{\text{Initial investment}}$$

Assuming that the cash flow calculated does not include the investment made in the project, a profitability index of 1 indicates breakeven.

Economic value	Economic value is a measure of the benefit that an economic actor can gain from either a good or service. It is generally measured relative to units of currency, and the interpretation is therefore 'what is the maximum amount of money a specific actor is willing and able to pay for the good or service'? The economic value of a good or service has puzzled economists since the beginning of the discipline. First, economists tried to estimate the value of a good to an individual alone, and extend that definition to goods which can be exchanged.
Economic Value Added	In corporate finance, Economic Value Added, is an estimate of a firm's economic profit - being the value created in excess of the required return of the company's investors . Quite simply, Economic Value Added is the profit earned by the firm less the cost of financing the firm's capital. The idea is that value is created when the return on the firm's economic capital employed is greater than the cost of that capital.
Pure economic loss	Economic loss is a term of art which refers to financial loss and damage suffered by a person such as can be seen only on a balance sheet rather than as physical injury to the person or destruction of property. There is a fundamental distinction between "pure economic loss" and "consequential economic loss", as pure economic loss occurs independent of any physical damage to the person or property of the victim. Usually, 'pure economic loss' in tort, particularly in negligence, is not recoverable as damages or otherwise.
Internal rate of return	The internal rate of return or economic rate of return (ERR) is a rate of return used in capital budgeting to measure and compare the profitability of investments. It is also called the discounted cash flow rate of return (DCFROR) or the rate of return (ROR). In the context of savings and loans the IRR is also called the effective interest rate.
Cash flow	Cash flow is the movement of money into or out of a business, project, or financial product. It is usually measured during a specified, limited period of time. Measurement of cash flow can be used for calculating other parameters that give information on a company's value and situation.

10. Capital Budgeting Techniques

CHAPTER QUIZ: KEY TERMS, PEOPLE, PLACES, CONCEPTS

1. _________, also known as present discounted value, is a future amount of money that has been discounted to reflect its current value, as if it existed today. The _________ is always less than or equal to the future value because money has interest-earning potential, a characteristic referred to as the time value of money. Time value can be described with the simplified phrase, "A dollar today is worth more than a dollar tomorrow".

a. Put-call parity
b. Quantitative investing
c. Present value
d. Range accrual

2. In economics, _________, _________ goods, or real _________ are those already-produced durable goods that are used in production of goods or services. The _________ goods are not significantly consumed, though they may depreciate in the production process. _________ is distinct from land in that _________ must itself be produced by human labor before it can be a factor of production.

a. Capital cost
b. Capital good
c. Capital
d. Capital outflow

3. _________ is a form of applied ethics or professional ethics that examines ethical principles and moral or ethical problems that arise in a business environment. It applies to all aspects of business conduct and is relevant to the conduct of individuals and entire organizations.

_________ has both normative and descriptive dimensions.

a. Hypernorms
b. Conspiracy of Fools
c. Business ethics
d. Jewish business ethics

4. Economic loss is a term of art which refers to financial loss and damage suffered by a person such as can be seen only on a balance sheet rather than as physical injury to the person or destruction of property. There is a fundamental distinction between "_________" and "consequential economic loss", as _________ occurs independent of any physical damage to the person or property of the victim. Usually, '_________' in tort, particularly in negligence, is not recoverable as damages or otherwise.

a. Pure economic loss
b. Coase theorem
c. Collegio Carlo Alberto
d. Complex structure theory in English law

5. _________ is the planning process used to determine whether an organization's long term investments such as new machinery, replacement machinery, new plants, new products, and research development projects are worth the funding of cash through the firm's capitalization structure (debt, equity or retained earnings). It is the process of allocating resources for major capital, or investment, expenditures. One of the primary goals of _________ investments is to increase the value of the firm to the shareholders.

a. Capital structure
b. Capitalization table
c. Capital budgeting
d. Cashflow matching

ANSWER KEY
10. Capital Budgeting Techniques

1. c
2. c
3. c
4. a
5. c

You can take the complete Chapter Practice Test

for 10. Capital Budgeting Techniques
on all key terms, persons, places, and concepts.

Online 99 Cents

http://www.JustTheFacts101.com

Use www.JustTheFacts101.com for all your study needs

including Facts101's online interactive problem solving labs in

chemistry, statistics, mathematics, and more.

11. Capital Budgeting Cash Flows and Risk Refinements

CHAPTER OUTLINE: KEY TERMS, PEOPLE, PLACES, CONCEPTS

- Capital budgeting
- Cash flow
- Sunk costs
- Opportunity cost
- Ask price
- Capital
- Foreign direct investment
- Book value
- Asset
- Price book
- Working capital
- Capital expenditure
- Cost
- Business ethics
- Scenario analysis
- Discount rate
- Capital asset
- Capital asset pricing model
- Security market line
- P3M3
- Net present value

11. Capital Budgeting Cash Flows and Risk Refinements

CHAPTER OUTLINE: KEY TERMS, PEOPLE, PLACES, CONCEPTS

_______________ Present value

_______________ Time value of an option

_______________ Rationing

CHAPTER HIGHLIGHTS & NOTES: KEY TERMS, PEOPLE, PLACES, CONCEPTS

Capital budgeting	Capital budgeting is the planning process used to determine whether an organization's long term investments such as new machinery, replacement machinery, new plants, new products, and research development projects are worth the funding of cash through the firm's capitalization structure (debt, equity or retained earnings). It is the process of allocating resources for major capital, or investment, expenditures. One of the primary goals of capital budgeting investments is to increase the value of the firm to the shareholders.
Cash flow	Cash flow is the movement of money into or out of a business, project, or financial product. It is usually measured during a specified, limited period of time. Measurement of cash flow can be used for calculating other parameters that give information on a company's value and situation.
Sunk costs	In economics and business decision-making, sunk costs are retrospective (past) costs that have already been incurred and cannot be recovered. Sunk costs are sometimes contrasted with prospective costs, which are future costs that may be incurred or changed if an action is taken. Both retrospective and prospective costs may be either fixed (continuous for as long as the business is in operation and unaffected by output volume) or variable (dependent on volume) costs.
Opportunity cost	In microeconomic theory, the opportunity cost of a choice is the value of the best alternative forgone, in a situation in which a choice needs to be made between several mutually exclusive alternatives given limited resources. Assuming the best choice is made, it is the 'cost' incurred by not enjoying the benefit that would be had by taking the second best choice available. The New Oxford American Dictionary defines it as 'the loss of potential gain from other alternatives when one alternative is chosen'.
Ask price	Ask price, also called offer price, offer, asking price, or simply ask, is the price a seller states she or he will accept for a good. The seller may qualify the stated asking price as firm or negotiable.

Capital	In economics, capital, capital goods, or real capital are those already-produced durable goods that are used in production of goods or services. The capital goods are not significantly consumed, though they may depreciate in the production process. Capital is distinct from land in that capital must itself be produced by human labor before it can be a factor of production.
Foreign direct investment	Foreign direct investment is a direct investment into production or business in a country by an individual or company in another country, either by buying a company in the target country or by expanding operations of an existing business in that country. Foreign direct investment is in contrast to portfolio investment which is a passive investment in the securities of another country such as stocks and bonds.
Book value	In accounting, book value or carrying value is the value of an asset according to its balance sheet account balance. For assets, the value is based on the original cost of the asset less any depreciation, amortization or impairment costs made against the asset. Traditionally, a company's book value is its total assets minus intangible assets and liabilities.
Asset	In financial accounting, assets are economic resources. Anything tangible or intangible that is capable of being owned or controlled to produce value and that is held to have positive economic value is considered an asset. Simply stated, assets represent value of ownership that can be converted into cash (although cash itself is also considered an asset).
Price book	In economics, a price book is a book in which the normal prices of an item are listed for all suppliers. This allows one to determine the lowest price possible. If a group of suppliers adhere to a particular price book, in other words, they set the prices of the price book artificially higher than the market clearing price, then they are 'fixing the price' of that item.
Working capital	Working capital is a financial metric which represents operating liquidity available to a business, organization or other entity, including governmental entity. Along with fixed assets such as plant and equipment, working capital is considered a part of operating capital. Net working capital is calculated as current assets minus current liabilities.
Capital expenditure	Capital expenditures are expenditures creating future benefits. A capital expenditure is incurred when a business spends money either to buy fixed assets or to add to the value of an existing fixed asset with a useful life extending beyond the taxable year.
Cost	In production, research, retail, and accounting, a cost is the value of money that has been used up to produce something, and hence is not available for use anymore. In business, the cost may be one of acquisition, in which case the amount of money expended to acquire it is counted as cost. In this case, money is the input that is gone in order to acquire the thing.

11. Capital Budgeting Cash Flows and Risk Refinements

CHAPTER HIGHLIGHTS & NOTES: KEY TERMS, PEOPLE, PLACES, CONCEPTS

Business ethics

Business ethics is a form of applied ethics or professional ethics that examines ethical principles and moral or ethical problems that arise in a business environment. It applies to all aspects of business conduct and is relevant to the conduct of individuals and entire organizations.

Business ethics has both normative and descriptive dimensions.

Scenario analysis

Scenario analysis is a process of analyzing possible future events by considering alternative possible outcomes (sometimes called 'alternative worlds'). Thus, the scenario analysis, which is a main method of projections, does not try to show one exact picture of the future. Instead, it presents consciously several alternative future developments.

Discount rate

The discount rate can mean•an interest rate a central bank charges depository institutions that borrow reserves from it, for example for the use of the Federal Reserve's discount window•the same as interest rate; the term 'discount' does not refer to the common meaning of the word, but to the meaning in computations of present value, e.g. net present value or discounted cash flow•the annual effective discount rate, which is the annual interest divided by the capital including that interest; this rate is lower than the interest rate; it corresponds to using the value after a year as the nominal value, and seeing the initial value as the nominal value minus a discount; it is used for Treasury Bills and similar financial instrumentsAnnual effective discount rate

The annual effective discount rate is the annual interest divided by the capital including that interest, which is the interest rate divided by 100% plus the interest rate. It is the annual discount factor to be applied to the future cash flow, to find the discount, subtracted from a future value to find the value one year earlier.

For example, suppose there is a government bond that sells for $95 and pays $100 in a year's time.

Capital asset

The term capital asset has three vaguely related definitions in specific accounting regimes and theories of economics. It is also used to refer to assets, including investments not held for sale, conversion or consumption# in the ordinary course of work or production or business. In the context of the capital asset pricing model it refers strictly to financialized instruments.

Capital asset pricing model

In finance, the capital asset pricing model is used to determine a theoretically appropriate required rate of return of an asset, if that asset is to be added to an already well-diversified portfolio, given that asset's non-diversifiable risk. The model takes into account the asset's sensitivity to non-diversifiable risk (also known as systematic risk or market risk), often represented by the quantity beta (ß) in the financial industry, as well as the expected return of the market and the expected return of a theoretical risk-free asset. Capital asset pricing model “suggests that an investor's cost of equity capital is determined by beta.” An extension to the Capital asset pricing model is the dual-beta model, which differentiates downside beta from upside beta.

Security market line	Security market line is the representation of the Capital asset pricing model. It displays the expected rate of return of an individual security as a function of systematic, non-diversifiable risk (its beta).
P3M3	P3M3, also known as the Portfolio, Programme and Project Management Maturity Model is a reference guide for structured best practice. It breaks down the broad disciplines of portfolio, programme and project management into a hierarchy of Key Process Areas (KPAs). The hierarchical approach enables organisations to assess their current capability and then plot a roadmap for improvement prioritised by those KPAs which will make the biggest impact on performance.
Net present value	In finance, the Net Present Value or Net Present Worth (NPW) of a time series of cash flows, both incoming and outgoing, is defined as the sum of the present values (PVs) of the individual cash flows of the same entity. In the case when all future cash flows are incoming (such as coupons and principal of a bond) and the only outflow of cash is the purchase price, the Net present value is simply the PV of future cash flows minus the purchase price (which is its own PV). Net present value is a central tool in discounted cash flow (DCF) analysis and is a standard method for using the time value of money to appraise long-term projects.
Present value	Present value, also known as present discounted value, is a future amount of money that has been discounted to reflect its current value, as if it existed today. The present value is always less than or equal to the future value because money has interest-earning potential, a characteristic referred to as the time value of money. Time value can be described with the simplified phrase, "A dollar today is worth more than a dollar tomorrow".
Time value of an option	In finance, the time value of an option is the premium a rational investor would pay over its current exercise value (intrinsic value), based on the probability it will increase in value before expiry. For an American option this value is always greater than zero in a fair market, thus an option is always worth more than its current exercise value. For a European option, the extrinsic value can be negative.
Rationing	Rationing is the controlled distribution of scarce resources, goods, or services. Rationing controls the size of the ration, one's allotted portion of the resources being distributed on a particular day or at a particular time. Rationing has long been used in the military, especially the navy, to make supplies or rations last for a defined duration, such as a voyage.

11. Capital Budgeting Cash Flows and Risk Refinements

CHAPTER QUIZ: KEY TERMS, PEOPLE, PLACES, CONCEPTS

1. _________ is a form of applied ethics or professional ethics that examines ethical principles and moral or ethical problems that arise in a business environment. It applies to all aspects of business conduct and is relevant to the conduct of individuals and entire organizations.

   _________ has both normative and descriptive dimensions.

   a. Business ethics
   b. Conspiracy of Fools
   c. Corporate Knights
   d. Jewish business ethics

2. _________ is the planning process used to determine whether an organization's long term investments such as new machinery, replacement machinery, new plants, new products, and research development projects are worth the funding of cash through the firm's capitalization structure (debt, equity or retained earnings). It is the process of allocating resources for major capital, or investment, expenditures. One of the primary goals of _________ investments is to increase the value of the firm to the shareholders.

   a. Capital structure
   b. Capital budgeting
   c. Cash is king
   d. Cashflow matching

3. _________ is a financial metric which represents operating liquidity available to a business, organization or other entity, including governmental entity. Along with fixed assets such as plant and equipment, _________ is considered a part of operating capital. Net _________ is calculated as current assets minus current liabilities.

   a. Negative carry
   b. Working capital
   c. granularity
   d. Price intelligence

4. _________ is the movement of money into or out of a business, project, or financial product. It is usually measured during a specified, limited period of time. Measurement of _________ can be used for calculating other parameters that give information on a company's value and situation.

   a. Cash flow forecasting
   b. Cash flow
   c. Checkoff
   d. Clean surplus accounting

5. . The term _________ has three vaguely related definitions in specific accounting regimes and theories of economics. It is also used to refer to assets, including investments not held for sale, conversion or consumption# in the ordinary course of work or production or business. In the context of the _________ pricing model it refers strictly to financialized instruments.

a. Capital asset
b. Commission
c. Conditional variance swap
d. Constant proportion portfolio insurance

ANSWER KEY

11. Capital Budgeting Cash Flows and Risk Refinements

---

1. a

2. b

3. b

4. b

5. a

You can take the complete Chapter Practice Test

for 11. Capital Budgeting Cash Flows and Risk Refinements
on all key terms, persons, places, and concepts.

Online 99 Cents

http://www.JustTheFacts101.com

Use www.JustTheFacts101.com for all your study needs

including Facts101's online interactive problem solving labs in

chemistry, statistics, mathematics, and more.

12. Leverage and Capital Structure

CHAPTER OUTLINE: KEY TERMS, PEOPLE, PLACES, CONCEPTS

- Leverage
- Earnings before interest and taxes
- Operating leverage
- Fixed cost
- Debt capital
- Capital
- Equity
- Debt ratio
- Agency cost
- Accounting profit
- Weight function
- Average cost
- Share capital
- Estimation
- Business risks
- Cash flow

12. Leverage and Capital Structure

CHAPTER HIGHLIGHTS & NOTES: KEY TERMS, PEOPLE, PLACES, CONCEPTS

Leverage	In negotiation, leverage is the ability to influence the other side to move closer to one's negotiating position. Types of leverage include positive leverage, negative leverage, and normative leverage. Normative Leverage Normative leverage is the application of general norms or the other party's standards and norms to advance one's own arguments for one's own good.
Earnings before interest and taxes	In accounting and finance, earnings before interest and taxes, is a measure of a firm's profit that excludes interest and income tax expenses. It is the difference between operating revenues and operating expenses. When a firm does not have non-operating income, then operating income is sometimes used as a synonym for Earnings before interest taxes and operating profit.
Operating leverage	Operating leverage is a measure of how revenue growth translates into growth in operating income. Leverage, and of how risky (volatile) a company's operating income is.
Fixed cost	In economics, fixed costs are business expenses that are not dependent on the level of goods or services produced by the business. They tend to be time-related, such as salaries or rents being paid per month, and are often referred to as overhead costs. This is in contrast to variable costs, which are volume-related (and are paid per quantity produced).
Debt capital	Debt capital is the capital that a business raises by taking out a loan. It is a loan made to a company that is normally repaid at some future date. Debt capital differs from equity or share capital because subscribers to debt capital do not become part owners of the business, but are merely creditors, and the suppliers of debt capital usually receive a contractually fixed annual percentage return on their loan, and this is known as the coupon rate.
Capital	In economics, capital, capital goods, or real capital are those already-produced durable goods that are used in production of goods or services. The capital goods are not significantly consumed, though they may depreciate in the production process. Capital is distinct from land in that capital must itself be produced by human labor before it can be a factor of production.
Equity	Equity or Economic equality, is the concept or idea of fairness in economics, particularly as to taxation or welfare economics. More specifically it may refer to equal life chances regardless of identity, to provide all citizens with a basic and equal minimum of income/goods/services or to increase funds and commitment for redistribution. Inequality and inequities have significantly increased in recent decades, possibly driven by the worldwide economic processes of globalisation, economic liberalisation and integration.

Debt ratio

Debt Ratio is a financial ratio that indicates the percentage of a company's assets that are provided via debt. It is the ratio of total debt (the sum of current liabilities and long-term liabilities) and total assets (the sum of current assets, fixed assets, and other assets such as 'goodwill').

$$\text{Debt ratio} = \frac{\text{Total Debt}}{\text{Total Assets}}$$

or alternatively:

$$\text{Debt ratio} = \frac{\text{Total Liability}}{\text{Total Assets}}$$

For example, a company with $2 million in total assets and $500,000 in total liabilities would have a debt ratio of 25%.

Agency cost

An agency cost is an economic concept concerning the cost to a 'principal', when the principal chooses or hires an 'agent' to act on its behalf. Because the two parties have different interests and the agent has more information, the principal cannot directly ensure that its agent is always acting in its (the principals') best interests.

Common examples of this cost include that borne by shareholders (the principal), when corporate management (the agent) buys other companies to expand its power, or spends money on wasteful pet projects, instead of maximizing the value of the corporation's worth; or by the voters of a politician's district (the principal) when the politician (the agent) passes legislation helpful to large contributors to their campaign rather than the voters.

Accounting profit

Accounting profit is the difference between price and the costs of bringing to market whatever it is that is accounted as an enterprise (whether by harvest, extraction, manufacture) in terms of the component costs of delivered goods and/or services and any operating or other expenses.

A key difficulty in measuring profit is in defining costs. Pure economic monetary profits can be zero or negative even in competitive equilibrium when accounted monetized costs exceed monetized price.

Weight function

A weight function is a mathematical device used when performing a sum, integral, or average to give some elements more 'weight' or influence on the result than other elements in the same set. They occur frequently in statistics and analysis, and are closely related to the concept of a measure. Weight functions can be employed in both discrete and continuous settings.

Average cost

In economics, average cost is equal to total cost divided by the number of goods produced (the output quantity, Q).

It is also equal to the sum of average variable costs (total variable costs divided by Q) plus average fixed costs (total fixed costs divided by Q). Average costs may be dependent on the time period considered (increasing production may be expensive or impossible in the short term, for example).

Share capital

Share capital or capital stock refers to the portion of a company's equity that has been obtained (or will be obtained) by trading stock to a shareholder for cash or an equivalent item of capital value. For example, a company can issue shares in exchange for computer servers, instead of purchasing the servers with cash.

The term has several meanings.

Estimation

Estimation is the process of finding an estimate, or approximation, which is a value that is usable for some purpose even if input data may be incomplete, uncertain, or unstable. The value is nonetheless usable because it is derived from the best information available. Typically, estimation involves 'using the value of a statistic derived from a sample to estimate the value of a corresponding population parameter'.

Business risks

Every business organization contains various risk elements while doing the business. Business risks implies uncertainty in profits or danger of loss and the events that could pose a risk due to some unforeseen events in future, which causes business to fail.

For example, an owner of a business may face different risks like in production,risks due to irregular supply of raw materials, machinery breakdown, labor unrest, etc.

Cash flow

Cash flow is the movement of money into or out of a business, project, or financial product. It is usually measured during a specified, limited period of time. Measurement of cash flow can be used for calculating other parameters that give information on a company's value and situation.

1. _________ is a measure of how revenue growth translates into growth in operating income. Leverage, and of how risky (volatile) a company's operating income is.

   a. Operating margin
   b. Operating leverage
   c. Bid-to-cover ratio
   d. Calmar ratio

2. In economics, _________s are business expenses that are not dependent on the level of goods or services produced by the business. They tend to be time-related, such as salaries or rents being paid per month, and are often referred to as overhead costs. This is in contrast to variable costs, which are volume-related (and are paid per quantity produced).

   a. Grenzplankostenrechnung
   b. Hedge accounting
   c. Holding cost
   d. Fixed cost

3. In negotiation, _________ is the ability to influence the other side to move closer to one's negotiating position.

   Types of _________ include positive _________, negative _________, and normative _________. Normative _________

   Normative _________ is the application of general norms or the other party's standards and norms to advance one's own arguments for one's own good.

   a. Location intelligence
   b. Loyalty marketing
   c. Leverage
   d. Market segmentation index

4. _________ is the capital that a business raises by taking out a loan. It is a loan made to a company that is normally repaid at some future date. _________ differs from equity or share capital because subscribers to _________ do not become part owners of the business, but are merely creditors, and the suppliers of _________ usually receive a contractually fixed annual percentage return on their loan, and this is known as the coupon rate.

   a. Debt overhang
   b. Debt rescheduling
   c. Debt capital
   d. Debt-for-nature swap

5. . In accounting and finance, _________, is a measure of a firm's profit that excludes interest and income tax expenses. It is the difference between operating revenues and operating expenses. When a firm does not have non-operating income, then operating income is sometimes used as a synonym for Earnings before interest taxes and operating profit.

   a. 7-day SEC yield

b. backwardation

c. Earnings before interest and taxes

d. Bank tax

ANSWER KEY
12. Leverage and Capital Structure

1. b
2. d
3. c
4. c
5. c

You can take the complete Chapter Practice Test

for 12. Leverage and Capital Structure
on all key terms, persons, places, and concepts.

Online 99 Cents

http://www.JustTheFacts101.com

Use www.JustTheFacts101.com for all your study needs

including Facts101's online interactive problem solving labs in

chemistry, statistics, mathematics, and more.

13. Payout Policy

CHAPTER OUTLINE: KEY TERMS, PEOPLE, PLACES, CONCEPTS

______	Clientele effect
______	Dividend
______	Dutch auction
______	Dividend payout ratio
______	Holder
______	Tender offer
______	Dividend reinvestment plan
______	Share price
______	Stock split
______	Reverse stock split

CHAPTER HIGHLIGHTS & NOTES: KEY TERMS, PEOPLE, PLACES, CONCEPTS

Clientele effect	The clientele effect is the idea that the set of investors attracted to a particular kind of security will affect the price of the security when policies or circumstances change. For instance, some investors want a company that doesn't pay dividends but instead invests that money in growing the business, whereas other investors prefer a stock that pays a high dividend, and still others want one that balances payout and reinvestment. If a company changes its dividend policy substantially, it is said to be subject to a clientele effect as some of its investors (its established clientele) decide to sell the security due to the change.
Dividend	A dividend is a payment made by a corporation to its shareholders, usually as a distribution of profits. When a corporation earns a profit or surplus, it can either re-invest it in the business (called retained earnings), or it can distribute it to shareholders. A corporation may retain a portion of its earnings and pay the remainder as a dividend.

13. Payout Policy

CHAPTER HIGHLIGHTS & NOTES: KEY TERMS, PEOPLE, PLACES, CONCEPTS

Dutch auction	A Dutch auction is a type of auction in which the auctioneer begins with a high asking price which is lowered until some participant is willing to accept the auctioneer's price, or a predetermined reserve price (the seller's minimum acceptable price) is reached. The winning participant pays the last announced price. This is also known as a so-called clock auction or an open-outcry descending-price auction.
Dividend payout ratio	Dividend payout ratio is the fraction of net income a firm pays to its stockholders in dividends: $$\text{Dividend payout ratio} = \frac{\text{Dividends}}{\text{Net Income for the same period}}$$ The part of the earnings not paid to investors is left for investment to provide for future earnings growth. Investors seeking high current income and limited capital growth prefer companies with high Dividend payout ratio. However investors seeking capital growth may prefer lower payout ratio because capital gains are taxed at a lower rate.
Holder	Holder is a term used in business law of any person that has in his custody a promissory note, bill of exchange or cheque. It should be entitled in his own name so as to possess and to recover the amount due from the parties concerned.
Tender offer	Tender offer is a corporate finance term denoting a type of takeover bid. The tender offer is a public, open offer or invitation (usually announced in a newspaper advertisement) by a prospective acquirer to all stockholders of a publicly traded corporation (the target corporation) to tender their stock for sale at a specified price during a specified time, subject to the tendering of a minimum and maximum number of shares. In a tender offer, the bidder contacts shareholders directly; the directors of the company may or may not have endorsed the tender offer proposal.
Dividend reinvestment plan	A dividend reinvestment program or dividend reinvestment plan is an equity investment option offered directly from the underlying company. The investor does not receive quarterly dividends directly as cash; instead, the investor's dividends are directly reinvested in the underlying equity. (The investor must still pay tax annually on his or her dividend income, whether it is received or reinvested).
Share price	A share price is the price of a single share of a number of saleable stocks of a company, derivative or other financial asset.
Stock split	A stock split or stock divide increases the number of shares in a public company. The price is adjusted such that the before and after market capitalization of the company remains the same and dilution does not occur. Options and warrants are included.

CHAPTER HIGHLIGHTS & NOTES: KEY TERMS, PEOPLE, PLACES, CONCEPTS

Reverse stock split	On a stock exchange, a reverse stock split or reverse split is a process by a company of issuing to each shareholder in that company a smaller number of new shares in proportion to that shareholder's original shares that are subsequently canceled. A reverse stock split is also called a stock merge. The reduction in the number of issued shares is accompanied by a proportional increase in the share price.

CHAPTER QUIZ: KEY TERMS, PEOPLE, PLACES, CONCEPTS

1. _________ is a term used in business law of any person that has in his custody a promissory note, bill of exchange or cheque. It should be entitled in his own name so as to possess and to recover the amount due from the parties concerned.

   a. Hundi
   b. Holder
   c. Jurisdictional strike
   d. Ladenschlussgesetz

2. A _________ is a payment made by a corporation to its shareholders, usually as a distribution of profits. When a corporation earns a profit or surplus, it can either re-invest it in the business (called retained earnings), or it can distribute it to shareholders. A corporation may retain a portion of its earnings and pay the remainder as a _________.

   a. Bonus share
   b. Common stock dividend
   c. Dividend
   d. Dividend cover

3. A _________ or stock divide increases the number of shares in a public company. The price is adjusted such that the before and after market capitalization of the company remains the same and dilution does not occur. Options and warrants are included.

   a. Stock split
   b. Strip financing
   c. Structural subordination
   d. Surplus note

4. . On a stock exchange, a _________ or reverse split is a process by a company of issuing to each shareholder in that company a smaller number of new shares in proportion to that shareholder's original shares that are subsequently canceled. A _________ is also called a stock merge. The reduction in the number of issued shares is accompanied by a proportional increase in the share price.

   a. Reverse stock split

b. Santa Claus rally
c. Scrip issue
d. preferred share

5. The _________ is the idea that the set of investors attracted to a particular kind of security will affect the price of the security when policies or circumstances change. For instance, some investors want a company that doesn't pay dividends but instead invests that money in growing the business, whereas other investors prefer a stock that pays a high dividend, and still others want one that balances payout and reinvestment. If a company changes its dividend policy substantially, it is said to be subject to a _________ as some of its investors (its established clientele) decide to sell the security due to the change.

a. CNBC
b. CNBC Ticker
c. Clientele effect
d. The Congressional Effect

ANSWER KEY
13. Payout Policy

1. b
2. c
3. a
4. a
5. c

You can take the complete Chapter Practice Test

for 13. Payout Policy
on all key terms, persons, places, and concepts.

Online 99 Cents

http://www.JustTheFacts101.com

Use www.JustTheFacts101.com for all your study needs including Facts101's online interactive problem solving labs in chemistry, statistics, mathematics, and more.

14. Working Capital and Current Assets Management

CHAPTER OUTLINE: KEY TERMS, PEOPLE, PLACES, CONCEPTS

Working capital

Insolvency

Cash conversion cycle

Stock market

Cash flow

Carrying cost

Total cost

Reorder point

Safety stock

Enterprise resource planning

Capital

Clearing

Cash concentration

Wire transfer

14. Working Capital and Current Assets Management

CHAPTER HIGHLIGHTS & NOTES: KEY TERMS, PEOPLE, PLACES, CONCEPTS

Working capital	Working capital is a financial metric which represents operating liquidity available to a business, organization or other entity, including governmental entity. Along with fixed assets such as plant and equipment, working capital is considered a part of operating capital. Net working capital is calculated as current assets minus current liabilities.
Insolvency	Insolvency is the inability of a debtor to pay their debt. Cash flow insolvency involves a lack of liquidity to pay debts as they fall due. Balance sheet insolvency involves having negative net assets --where liabilities exceed assets.
Cash conversion cycle	In management accounting, the cash conversion cycle measures how long a firm will be deprived of cash if it increases its investment in resources in order to expand customer sales. It is thus a measure of the liquidity risk entailed by growth. However, shortening the Cash conversion cycle creates its own risks: while a firm could even achieve a negative Cash conversion cycle by collecting from customers before paying suppliers, a policy of strict collections and lax payments is not always sustainable.
Stock market	A stock market or equity market is a public entity for the trading of company stock (shares) and derivatives at an agreed price; these are securities listed on a stock exchange as well as those only traded privately. The size of the world stock market was estimated at about $36.6 trillion at the beginning of October 2008. The total world derivatives market has been estimated at about $791 trillion face or nominal value, 11 times the size of the entire world economy. The value of the derivatives market, because it is stated in terms of notional values, cannot be directly compared to a stock or a fixed income security, which traditionally refers to an actual value.
Cash flow	Cash flow is the movement of money into or out of a business, project, or financial product. It is usually measured during a specified, limited period of time. Measurement of cash flow can be used for calculating other parameters that give information on a company's value and situation.
Carrying cost	In marketing, carrying cost refers to the total cost of holding inventory. This includes warehousing costs such as rent, utilities and salaries, financial costs such as opportunity cost, and inventory costs related to perishability, shrinkage and insurance. When there are no transaction costs for shipment, carrying costs are minimized when no excess inventory is held at all, as in a Just In Time production system.
Total cost	In economics, and cost accounting, total cost describes the total economic cost of production and is made up of variable costs, which vary according to the quantity of a good produced and include inputs such as labor and raw materials, plus fixed costs, which are independent of the quantity of a good produced and include inputs (capital) that cannot be varied in the short term, such as buildings and machinery.

Total cost in economics includes the total opportunity cost of each factor of production as part of its fixed or variable costs.

The rate at which total cost changes as the amount produced changes is called marginal cost.

Reorder point	The reorder point is the level of inventory when an order should be made with suppliers to bring the inventory up by the Economic order quantity ('EOQ').
Safety stock	Safety stock is a term used by logisticians to describe a level of extra stock that is maintained to mitigate risk of stockouts (shortfall in raw material or packaging) due to uncertainties in supply and demand. Adequate safety stock levels permit business operations to proceed according to their plans. Safety stock is held when there is uncertainty in the demand level or lead time for the product; it serves as an insurance against stockouts.
Enterprise resource planning	Enterprise resource planning is a cross-functional enterprise system driven by an integrated suite of software modules that supports the basic internal business processes of a company. Enterprise resource planning gives a company an integrated real-time view of its core business processes such as production, order processing, and inventory management, tied together by Enterprise resource planning applications software and a common database maintained by a database management systems. Enterprise resource planning systems track business resources (such as cash, raw materials, and production capacity) and the status of commitments made by the business (such as customer orders, purchase orders, and employee payroll), no matter which department (manufacturing, purchasing, sales, accounting, and so on) has entered the data into the system.
Capital	In economics, capital, capital goods, or real capital are those already-produced durable goods that are used in production of goods or services. The capital goods are not significantly consumed, though they may depreciate in the production process. Capital is distinct from land in that capital must itself be produced by human labor before it can be a factor of production.
Clearing	In banking and finance, clearing denotes all activities from the time a commitment is made for a transaction until it is settled. Clearing is necessary because the speed of trades is much faster than the cycle time for completing the underlying transaction. In its widest sense clearing involves the management of post-trading, pre-settlement credit exposures, to ensure that trades are settled in accordance with market rules, even if a buyer or seller should become insolvent prior to settlement.
Cash concentration	Cash concentration is the transfer of funds from diverse accounts into a central account to improve the efficiency of cash management. The consolidation of cash into a single account allows a company to maintain smaller cash balances overall, and to identify excess cash available for short term investments.

14. Working Capital and Current Assets Management

CHAPTER HIGHLIGHTS & NOTES: KEY TERMS, PEOPLE, PLACES, CONCEPTS

	The cash available in different bank accounts are pooled into a master account.The advantages of cash concentration are 1) Cash control 2) Cash visibility For example, you have 2 bank accounts (i.e. Rizabank and Bank Islam).
Wire transfer	Wire transfer or credit transfer is a method of electronic funds transfer from one person or institution to another. A wire transfer can be made from one bank account to another bank account or through a transfer of cash at a cash office, such as Western Union. Wire transfer systems are intended to provide more individualized transactions than bulk payment systems such as the US ACH and Check21 systems.

CHAPTER QUIZ: KEY TERMS, PEOPLE, PLACES, CONCEPTS

1. _________ or credit transfer is a method of electronic funds transfer from one person or institution to another. A _________ can be made from one bank account to another bank account or through a transfer of cash at a cash office, such as Western Union. _________ systems are intended to provide more individualized transactions than bulk payment systems such as the US ACH and Check21 systems.

   a. Wirecard
   b. XIPWIRE
   c. Wire transfer
   d. Zimswitch

2. _________ is a financial metric which represents operating liquidity available to a business, organization or other entity, including governmental entity. Along with fixed assets such as plant and equipment, _________ is considered a part of operating capital. Net _________ is calculated as current assets minus current liabilities.

   a. Negative carry
   b. Positive carry
   c. Working capital
   d. Jimmy Carter

3. . In economics, _________, _________ goods, or real _________ are those already-produced durable goods that are used in production of goods or services. The _________ goods are not significantly consumed, though they may depreciate in the production process. _________ is distinct from land in that _________ must itself be produced by human labor before it can be a factor of production.

   a. Capital cost
   b. Capital
   c. Capital levy

4. _________ is the inability of a debtor to pay their debt. Cash flow _________ involves a lack of liquidity to pay debts as they fall due. Balance sheet _________ involves having negative net assets--where liabilities exceed assets.

a. Internal debt
b. Insolvency
c. Bailout
d. Borrowing base

5. In management accounting, the _________ measures how long a firm will be deprived of cash if it increases its investment in resources in order to expand customer sales. It is thus a measure of the liquidity risk entailed by growth. However, shortening the _________ creates its own risks: while a firm could even achieve a negative _________ by collecting from customers before paying suppliers, a policy of strict collections and lax payments is not always sustainable.

a. Cash flow return on investment
b. Cash conversion cycle
c. CROCI
d. Current ratio

ANSWER KEY

14. Working Capital and Current Assets Management

---

1. c

2. c

3. b

4. b

5. b

You can take the complete Chapter Practice Test

for 14. Working Capital and Current Assets Management

on all key terms, persons, places, and concepts.

Online 99 Cents

http://www.JustTheFacts101.com

Use www.JustTheFacts101.com for all your study needs

including Facts101's online interactive problem solving labs in

chemistry, statistics, mathematics, and more.

15. Current Liabilities Management

CHAPTER OUTLINE: KEY TERMS, PEOPLE, PLACES, CONCEPTS

- Accounts payable
- Cash conversion cycle
- Interest rate
- Prime rate
- Cash flow
- Line of credit
- Revolving credit
- Commercial paper
- Secondary market
- Commercial finance
- Accounts receivable
- Collateral
- Warehouse receipt
- Stock market

Accounts payable	Accounts payable is money owed by a business to its suppliers and shown on its Balance Sheet as a liability. An accounts payable is recorded in the Account Payable sub-ledger at the time an invoice is vouchered for payment. Vouchered, or vouched, means that an invoice is approved for payment and has been recorded in the General Ledger or AP subledger as an outstanding,or open, liability because it has not been paid.
Cash conversion cycle	In management accounting, the cash conversion cycle measures how long a firm will be deprived of cash if it increases its investment in resources in order to expand customer sales. It is thus a measure of the liquidity risk entailed by growth. However, shortening the Cash conversion cycle creates its own risks: while a firm could even achieve a negative Cash conversion cycle by collecting from customers before paying suppliers, a policy of strict collections and lax payments is not always sustainable.
Interest rate	An interest rate is the rate at which interest is paid by borrowers for the use of money that they borrow from a lender. Specifically, the interest rate is a percent of principal (P) paid a certain amount of times (m) per period (usually quoted per annum). For example, a small company borrows capital from a bank to buy new assets for its business, and in return the lender receives interest at a predetermined interest rate for deferring the use of funds and instead lending it to the borrower.
Prime rate	Prime rate or prime lending rate is a term applied in many countries to reference an interest rate used by banks. The term originally indicated the rate of interest at which banks lent to favored customers, i.e., those with good credit, though this is no longer always the case. Some variable interest rates may be expressed as a percentage above or below prime rate.
Cash flow	Cash flow is the movement of money into or out of a business, project, or financial product. It is usually measured during a specified, limited period of time. Measurement of cash flow can be used for calculating other parameters that give information on a company's value and situation.
Line of credit	A line of credit is any credit source extended to a government, business or individual by a bank or other financial institution. A line of credit may take several forms, such as overdraft protection, demand loan, special purpose, export packing credit, term loan, discounting, purchase of commercial bills, traditional revolving credit card account, etc. It is effectively a source of funds that can readily be tapped at the borrower's discretion.
Revolving credit	Revolving credit is a type of credit that does not have a fixed number of payments, in contrast to installment credit. Credit cards are an example of revolving credit used by consumers. Corporate revolving credit facilities are typically used to provide liquidity for a company's day-to-day operations.
Commercial paper	In the global money market, commercial paper is an unsecured promissory note with a fixed maturity of no more than 270 days.

Commercial paper is a money-market security issued (sold) by large corporations to get money to meet short term debt obligations (for example, payroll), and is only backed by an issuing bank or corporation's promise to pay the face amount on the maturity date specified on the note. Since it is not backed by collateral, only firms with excellent credit ratings from a recognized rating agency will be able to sell their commercial paper at a reasonable price.

Secondary market

The secondary market, also called aftermarket, is the financial market in which previously issued financial instruments such as stock, bonds, options, and futures are bought and sold. Another frequent usage of 'secondary market' is to refer to loans which are sold by a mortgage bank to investors such as Fannie Mae and Freddie Mac.

The term 'secondary market' is also used to refer to the market for any used goods or assets, or an alternative use for an existing product or asset where the customer base is the second market (for example, corn has been traditionally used primarily for food production and feedstock, but a 'second' or 'third' market has developed for use in ethanol production).

Commercial finance

In the United States, commercial finance is the function of offering loans to businesses. Commercial financing is generally offered by a bank or other lender. Most commercial banks offer commercial financing, and the loans are either secured by business assets or alternatively can be unsecured, where the lender relies of the cash flows of the business to repay the facility.

Accounts receivable

Accounts receivable are a legally enforceable claim for payment to a business by its customer/ clients for goods supplied and/or services rendered in execution of the customer's order. These are generally in the form of invoices raised by the business and delivered to the customer for payment within an agreed time frame. Accounts receivable are shown in the balance sheet as asset..

Collateral

In lending agreements, collateral is a borrower's pledge of specific property to a lender, to secure repayment of a loan. The collateral serves as protection for a lender against a borrower's default - that is, any borrower failing to pay the principal and interest under the terms of a loan obligation. If a borrower does default on a loan (due to insolvency or other event), that borrower forfeits (gives up) the property pledged as collateral - and the lender then becomes the owner of the collateral.

Warehouse receipt

A warehouse receipt is a document that provides proof of ownership of commodities (e.g., bars of copper) that are stored in a warehouse, vault, or depository for safekeeping.

Warehouse receipts may be negotiable or non-negotiable. Negotiable warehouse receipts allow transfer of ownership of that commodity without having to deliver the physical commodity.

Stock market

A stock market or equity market is a public entity for the trading of company stock (shares) and derivatives at an agreed price; these are securities listed on a stock exchange as well as those only traded privately.

The size of the world stock market was estimated at about $36.6 trillion at the beginning of October 2008. The total world derivatives market has been estimated at about $791 trillion face or nominal value, 11 times the size of the entire world economy. The value of the derivatives market, because it is stated in terms of notional values, cannot be directly compared to a stock or a fixed income security, which traditionally refers to an actual value.

CHAPTER QUIZ: KEY TERMS, PEOPLE, PLACES, CONCEPTS

1. _________ is the movement of money into or out of a business, project, or financial product. It is usually measured during a specified, limited period of time. Measurement of _________ can be used for calculating other parameters that give information on a company's value and situation.

   a. Cash flow forecasting
   b. Cash flow
   c. Checkoff
   d. Clean surplus accounting

2. The _________, also called aftermarket, is the financial market in which previously issued financial instruments such as stock, bonds, options, and futures are bought and sold. Another frequent usage of '_________' is to refer to loans which are sold by a mortgage bank to investors such as Fannie Mae and Freddie Mac.

   The term '_________' is also used to refer to the market for any used goods or assets, or an alternative use for an existing product or asset where the customer base is the second market (for example, corn has been traditionally used primarily for food production and feedstock, but a 'second' or 'third' market has developed for use in ethanol production).

   a. Short
   b. Secondary market
   c. Securities Industry and Financial Markets Association
   d. Sola Access Information Language

3. . In lending agreements, _________ is a borrower's pledge of specific property to a lender, to secure repayment of a loan. The _________ serves as protection for a lender against a borrower's default - that is, any borrower failing to pay the principal and interest under the terms of a loan obligation. If a borrower does default on a loan (due to insolvency or other event), that borrower forfeits (gives up) the property pledged as _________ - and the lender then becomes the owner of the _________.

   a. Compulsive buying disorder
   b. Cost of funds index

c. Courtesy signing
d. Collateral

4. _________ is money owed by a business to its suppliers and shown on its Balance Sheet as a liability. An _________ is recorded in the Account Payable sub-ledger at the time an invoice is vouchered for payment. Vouchered, or vouched, means that an invoice is approved for payment and has been recorded in the General Ledger or AP subledger as an outstanding,or open, liability because it has not been paid.

a. Double-entry
b. Accounts payable
c. University of Strathclyde
d. American Bar Association

5. A _________ is any credit source extended to a government, business or individual by a bank or other financial institution. A _________ may take several forms, such as overdraft protection, demand loan, special purpose, export packing credit, term loan, discounting, purchase of commercial bills, traditional revolving credit card account, etc. It is effectively a source of funds that can readily be tapped at the borrower's discretion.

a. Loan agreement
b. Line of credit
c. Loan guarantee
d. Loan sale

ANSWER KEY
15. Current Liabilities Management

---

1. b
2. b
3. d
4. b
5. b

You can take the complete Chapter Practice Test

for 15. Current Liabilities Management
on all key terms, persons, places, and concepts.

Online 99 Cents

http://www.JustTheFacts101.com

Use www.JustTheFacts101.com for all your study needs

including Facts101's online interactive problem solving labs in

chemistry, statistics, mathematics, and more.

Other Facts101 e-Books and Tests

Want More?
JustTheFacts101.com...

Jtf101.com provides the outlines and highlights of your textbooks, just like this e-StudyGuide, but also gives you the PRACTICE TESTS, and other exclusive study tools for all of your textbooks.

Learn More. *Just click http://www.JustTheFacts101.com/*

CPSIA information can be obtained at www.ICGtesting.com
Printed in the USA
BVOW09s0226050116

431734BV00037B/124/P